The Story of New Hampshire

THE STORY OF
NEW HAMPSHIRE

J. DUANE SQUIRES
Drawings by Laurence R. Webster

D. VAN NOSTRAND COMPANY, INC.
Princeton, New Jersey

TORONTO   NEW YORK   LONDON

D. VAN NOSTRAND COMPANY, INC.
120 Alexander St., Princeton, New Jersey (*Principal office*)
24 West 40 Street, New York 18, New York

D. VAN NOSTRAND COMPANY, LTD.
358, Kensington High Street, London, W.14, England

D. VAN NOSTRAND COMPANY, LTD.
25 Hollinger Road, Toronto 16, Canada

Library of Congress Catalog Card No. 64–19835

PRINTED IN THE UNITED STATES OF AMERICA

To My Beloved Grandchildren
JAMES AUSTIN SQUIRES
ELIZABETH ARLENE SQUIRES
VERNON PELLETT SQUIRES
and any others who yet may be

Contents

Illustrations at Chapter Openings

Introduction

In the December 24, 1962 issue of the noted magazine, *Sports Illustrated,* Catherine Drinker Bowen paid a glowing tribute to the American past. Her title was "Our Heritage of Boldness." In lucid words Mrs. Bowen showed clearly that the basic American trait for more than three centuries has been boldness in dreaming, boldness in persistence, boldness in accomplishment.

I think that this is a true assessment of the American experience as a whole, and I know that it is valid for New Hampshire history in particular. For in this little State, one of the half dozen smallest in the mighty U.S.A. of fifty states, there have been countless instances of bold Americans tackling their problems and mastering them. It took boldness to settle in New Hampshire three hundred years ago, to face the bleak winters, and, until 1763, the perils from New France to the north. It took boldness to wrest from the rugged soil and the dense forests the means of livelihood. It took boldness to master the steam engine and link it to the steamboat, the steam railway, and the power machines of the emerging factories. It took boldness to see in later years the possibility of harnessing the rivers to produce electricity and to run the huge transmission lines from mountains to seaboard.

New Hampshire people for three centuries have revealed as in a mirror the main currents of American life. First there was an overwhelming dependence on agriculture and such kindred vocations as fishing and lumbering. Then came the development of the extractive industries and the rise of manufacturing. And in the last century we have seen the influx of the tourist, the growth of suburbia, the impact of electricity and electronics, and the effects of the "Cold War" on the life and economy of the State.

New Hampshire is an old state, going back to 1623. It has a lively sense of the importance of tradition in human life, a keen awareness of knowing something of the value of past experience. New Hampshire is a small state. It is possible to study its past without being overwhelmed by an infinity of detail. New Hampshire is a well-balanced state, with many economic "irons in the fire." It is not provincial or narrow in the way that a commonwealth with only one basic manner of making a living tends to become. It has been well said that so-called liberals are always being surprised at the way people behave, while so-called conservatives are constantly being shocked by the same facts. New Hampshire is fortunate in that it has relatively few of the extremes in either of these groups, and has always been able to face the future with common sense and some humor.

Not by accident was the beautiful stage play by Thorton Wilder entitled *Our Town* laid in New Hampshire. Where else could it better have been laid? It is not by chance that Stephen Vincent Benét told one of New Hampshire's most famous stories in his *The Devil and Daniel Webster*. It is not mere fortuitous circumstance that made Hawthorne's "The Great Stone Face" seem appropriate for this State. It is not happenstance that Robert Frost, and Augustus St. Gaudens, and Daniel Chester French, and Edward MacDowell lived much of their lives in New Hampshire. All these men caught the spirit of the state in their works,—a spirit of rugged independence, delightful whimsy, and a great boldness of standing on one's own two feet.

Cornelius Weygandt once described New Hampshire folk as the "merriest of the Puritans." I think he was right. Whether in summer activities like the annual Fair of the New Hampshire League of Arts and Crafts, or in winter Snow Carnivals, or in spring festivities like "sugaring off" parties, or in the Fall

Foliage Tours, there is always something blithe and gay afoot in New Hampshire. The people are serious but not somber; they are whimsical but not frivolous; they are thoughtful but not pedantic; they are ingenious but not impractical. New Hampshire is a good state in which to live, and its history is well worth telling and reading.

J. DUANE SQUIRES

New London, New Hampshire

1. *Before the White Men Came*

Long before anyone lived in New Hampshire, there was activity within its present borders. It is generally agreed by modern students that the last great ice sheets, or glaciers, melted away not much more than 15,000 years ago. These enormous masses of ice came down from what is today called Canada, moving in a direction from northwest to southeast. They ground over the tops of our mountains, scratching the hardest rocks with marks which are still visible today, and pushing along the millions of stones and boulders which covered so much of the land when the white men first came. They scraped out the "notches" of the White Mountains, made the lakes and ponds which are found throughout the state today, and left the deposits of sand and gravel so useful to modern road builders.

These glaciers were really enormous natural bulldozers. The

ice sheet was perhaps a mile thick in places, and the weight of it was so large that it is hard even to calculate. It did not lie quietly on the earth's surface but crept slowly across the country. Every hill, mountain, slough, swamp, pond, lake, bog, marsh, hummock, hollow, or area of good and bad soil is the direct result of these ice movements. Parts of what we today call Mount Ascutney in Vermont have been found in Hinsdale, Fitzwilliam, and Rindge in modern New Hampshire. Pieces of the Red Hill in Moultonborough and bits from the Ossipee Mountains have been found in Maine. The largest single rock in New Hampshire, the so-called Madison Boulder, was dropped there by the glacier. The curious hills known as "drumlins" found in the region around Peterborough and Jaffrey are glacial remains. So also are the queer "potholes" scoured in solid rock seen in many places in the state.

After the glaciers began to melt away, plants and animals slowly appeared. By the time the white men discovered the New World, there were more than a hundred kinds of trees growing in New Hampshire, the white pine being especially important. It has been estimated that in 1600 all but 900 square miles of the present state was forested. From the great forests was to come much of the livelihood of early New Hampshire. First of all, they furnished wood for fuel. It may be forgotten today, but as late as 1900 most people in New Hampshire heated their homes in winter with wood and cooked their food over wood fires. The ashes of this fuel furnished fertilizer for the gardens and became the basic stuff out of which soap was made. Secondly, the great forests furnished lumber from which houses could be built. From the forests came woods which could be carved into dishes, made into furniture, bent into baskets, and used in hundreds of other ways. The woods provided the materials from which the frontier settlers often constructed log cabins. Even more important, perhaps, was the use to which the white pine forests were put in furnishing the masts for the great sailing ships of early days.

2

The largest ships of that period used masts more than a hundred feet in height, and there were thousands of trees in New Hampshire suited for such purposes.

In addition to the varied and useful forest growth, shrubs and flowering plants were found in almost all parts of New Hampshire. These included bushes like blueberry, raspberry, wild cherry, blackberry, and wild grapes. Lovely trees, azaleas, rhododendrons, and mountain laurel made the forest beautiful in the summertime. Useful herbs were abundant, and later were used for medicine: thyme, anise, mullein, and pennyroyal. In the high mountains grew many amazing tiny plants which today are called Alpine, meaning that they are like the plants that grow in the mountains of Switzerland.

Among the animals that were abundant in the state in the early days were deer, bear, moose, panthers, beaver, otter, and wolves. As late as 1787 New Hampshire was regarded by people in other parts of the United States as a wonderful hunting ground, and even today there is a great exhibit of our wild animals in the American Museum of Natural History in New York City. Beaver were trapped both by the Indians and by the white people later as a valuable source of fur. Deer meat, or venison, was a staple food both for Indians and whites.

Dozens of kinds of fish grew in the rivers and lakes of the state or flourished along the seacoast. In the two chief rivers of New Hampshire, the Merrimack and the Connecticut, migratory fish were abundant beyond belief today. On the Merrimack, for instance, every spring huge masses of shad and salmon came up the river to spawn. At modern Franklin, the shad took the branch that today is called the Winnipesaukee River, while the salmon kept on going straight north into the Pemigewasset River. In the early days these rivers were alive with sturgeon and eels. Sturgeon as long as twelve feet were taken in the Merrimack River by the Indians and the first white settlers. So abundant were eels in the Merrimack that the early settlers around modern Manchester depended on them for a large part of their diet. A little poem was written about this, which ran as follows:

> *From the eels they formed their food in chief*
> *And eels were called the Derryfield beef.*

This tremendous growth of fish in the rivers was destined to be spoiled by the modern pollution of these streams and by the later building of many dams for power purposes.

Along the seacoast there were huge schools of cod, haddock, pollack, mackerel, and flounder, and abundant quantities of such queer creatures as lobsters and clams. In the autumn great flocks of wild geese, ducks, and other waterfowl passed over New Hampshire, many of them stopping to rest on the coastal marshes and bays. No wonder that along the ocean and at such inland places as The Weirs, both the Indians and later the white people loved to go hunting and fishing.

Wild bird life was equally abundant in New Hampshire. Over 200 kinds of songbirds were native to the state. Vast flocks of wild pigeons, sufficient to darken the sky, often swept over the forests. Wild turkeys were numerous in the woods, as were grouse, woodcock, and other birds. The first white explorers that came to New Hampshire were greatly impressed with the wonderful variety and abundance of all manner of wild life in the new land, and often wrote about it.

These wild creatures ranged over a remarkably varied landscape. What is today New Hampshire had just eighteen miles of seacoast, which touches the Atlantic Ocean. From this low point, the land rises until on the top of Mount Washington it is more than 6200 feet high. There are eight mountains in New Hampshire more than a mile in height, and more than 150 reach above a half mile in height. There are five chief drainage basins in the state. The largest of these is the Merrimack Valley, which covers a little more than a third of New Hampshire. The next largest river basin is that of the Connecticut. The New Hampshire part of this river valley is just under a third of the total area of the state. The other parts of New Hampshire fall into three regions: the short coastal rivers like the Oyster, Exeter, Cocheco; the Saco; and the Androscoggin.

There are more than 1300 bodies of water in New Hampshire, described as lakes or ponds. The largest of these is the great lake called Winnipesaukee, one of the largest fresh-water bodies in the entire United States entirely within the borders of one state. Other important lakes are Squam, Winnisquam, Sunapee, Mascoma, Ossipee, and Newfound. Modern man, of course, by damming the rivers, has made many new lakes where none existed in the early days. These lakes have always been valuable as sources of food, as ways of travel, and in modern times as places for recreation.

About ten miles off the shore line at Portsmouth are the bleak islands called the Isles of Shoals. There are eight or nine islands, depending upon whether one is counting at high or at low tide. Appledore, Duck, Malaga, Smuttynose, and Cedar Islands belong to Maine. Star, Lunging, White, and Seavey Islands are a part of New Hampshire. Appledore, named after a little town in England, is the largest of the nine islands, but even so is barely a half mile wide at its greatest extent.

New Hampshire did not include among its natural resources any such kinds of ready wealth as the coal mines of Pennsylvania or the gold mines of California. But there was a vast amount of clay which could be baked into bricks and other pottery products. There certainly was an endless supply of granite—hence the nickname of the state—and from the earliest times this hard and valuable rock was split and quarried. There were such other minerals as soapstone for sinks; mica for various uses; quartz for glassmaking; "bog iron" in many places such as Gilmanton; and semi-precious stones like garnet or topaz. An important source of fertilizer was the peat found in bogs and swampy places. Salt was a vital resource in the days when there was no easy way to preserve food, and the ocean waters off New Hampshire's coast provided ample supplies of this material.

By the year 1600, when the first white men were beginning to sail along the coast line of New Hampshire, the native peoples who were to be called "Indians" had found the area and were living in various parts of the modern state. Despite the terrible things that happened later, these "red men," or Indians were for the most part friendly and peaceful when the white men first met them. There were not as many of them as people today imagine. Probably not more than 5000 Indians in all lived within the borders of present-day New Hampshire. They were "woods Indians"; that is, they lived primarily off the resources and life of the forest, and they had learned very well how to do this and how to survive the long cold winters of New England.

The New Hampshire Indians belonged to a group known as Algonkian. This large group of tribes was in turn divided into the Abnaki and the Pennacook tribes. The Abnaki Indians lived in the eastern portion of modern New Hampshire, along the Maine borders, including the tribes known as the Ossipees and the Pequawkets. The Pennacook Indians included such tribes as the Amoskeags, the Nashuas, the Piscataquas, the Souhegans, and the Squamscots.

These Indians lived primarily on the products of Nature as the wilderness furnished these to them. Their villages varied in population from fifty to 200 people, and normally were moved from one location to another every few years. In the Merrimack Valley alone, more than fifty sites of old Indian villages have been uncovered by modern students. From these old sites have come arrowheads, spearheads, pottery, pipes, and tomahawks. The largest of all Indian villages in New Hampshire was located at the place now called The Weirs. Here the Indians congregated to net fish as they came in or out of Lake Winnipesaukee.

It is hard to overstate the importance of the Indians and their knowledge to the early white men. It was the Indians who had learned how to clear and cultivate the forest lands. The Indians had learned how to extract maple sirup and sugar from the sap of the maple tree. The Indians had learned how to strip the bark off a birch tree and make the wonderfully light and useful craft known as a canoe. The Indians had invented snowshoes, moccasins, and traps for wild animals. The Indians had learned to distinguish one herb from another and to know which were useful and which were harmful to human beings. The Indians had found and cultivated such crops as squash, pumpkins, and many kinds of beans. The Indians had found the best ways of travel through the wild country and had made trails which the white men were to follow. In short, the Indians were the teachers to the white people from Europe and taught them many things which they might never have found out for themselves.

Perhaps the most valuable agricultural contribution the Indians were to make to the white men was their knowledge and cultivation of maize, or "Indian corn." This remarkable plant is native to the Western hemisphere and had never been known to white people before the discovery of America. The Indians had learned to grow many varieties, and it was their cereal staff of life. They had learned that frost is the enemy of corn, and that corn should not be planted in the spring until the leaves of the "white oak are as big as the ear of a mouse." They had learned how to dry the kernels to form parched corn. They had learned to pound it in a mortar until it had softened; then they called it "hominy." The Indians made mortars for this process, sometimes out of wood, sometimes out of stone. Occasionally they used a glacial pothole as a natural mortar. They had learned to mix corn with various kinds of beans and to call the result "succotash." They had even learned how to pop corn.

Maize, or Indian corn, was grown all the way from South America to New England. The Indians knew the value of fertile soil for their crop, but the problem of cutting down the trees to open up space for cultivation was a great one. One way

7

they devised was to "girdle" a tree near the base, shutting off the flow of sap so that the tree would die. Then, when it was dry and brittle, it could be burned or perhaps toppled over and dragged away. Thus they made their little fields, and on these clearings in the woods they grew their corn. After these fields had begun to lose their fertility, the Indians would move on to another site and begin all over again.

When the white men came they often noted these old clearings and wondered how such places happened to be free of trees. More often than not, these were the "old fields" of the Indians who had once lived there. At least eight of our modern New Hampshire communities—Nashua, Manchester, Concord, Franklin, The Weirs, Hooksett, Suncook, and Laconia—are built upon the site of old Indian villages of this type.

Of all the contributions of the Indians to the white people, however, none was more important than the birchbark canoe. This remarkable little craft was the invention of the Algonkian Indians, and especially of that group which lived in New England. Since these Indians were often migratory hunters, and since their native lands included a complex network of lakes and rivers, they needed a type of boat which would carry a good burden, yet be light enough to be transported easily from one waterway to another. Or, as we would say, they needed a craft which could be portaged. The birchbark canoe fitted all these requirements. It was made by skilled workmen from the bark of a single big birch tree, which was stripped from the trunk and then molded over ribs of cedar wood. It was sewed together at each end by thongs, and all leaky places were stopped by pitch. No one knows the name of the tribal inventor or inventors who devised the birchbark canoe, but the white men later on flattered these Indians by imitating their work.

The Indians unfortunately lived in a way that made them come to feel enmity to the white settlers, just as the white settlers soon came to feel anger against the Indians. Thus a long and sad period of warfare between white and red men came about, spoiling the originally friendly relations which had existed between the two kinds of people. But we must not forget how important all this Indian knowledge was to the first white settlers and how much they really owed to it.

Today the Indians are completely gone from New Hampshire. But they have left upon the land a great many names which still ring in our ears. There are towns like Penacook, Suncook, and Contoocook. There are names of rivers like Merrimack, Soucook, and Piscataquog. In the mountain areas the names of such old Indian chiefs as Wonalancet, Chocorua, and Kancamagus appear on modern maps. The Indians liked words which ended in *cook* or *ook;* hence some of the modern place names in New Hampshire have these endings. They also liked words which ended in *auke* or *ack;* hence we have still such names as Moosilauke or Merrimack. And they liked words with *squam* in them; hence we have such modern names as Winnisquam, Squamscott, and even Mascoma.

A recent study of the Indians of New Hampshire lists the following places where you can examine the many relics which have been dug up in modern times:

Auburn: The Griffin Free Library has more than 250 artifacts from the vicinity of Massabesic Lake, and twenty-two roller pestles.

Hanover: The Dartmouth College Museum has a large collection of Indian materials, many of them drawn from New Hampshire places.

Manchester: The Manchester Historic Association has roller pestles, axes, adzes, gouges, knives, points, arrowheads, and also a soapstone dish with four handles.

The Institute of Arts and Sciences has a fine collection of pottery, ornaments, adzes, axes, knives, war paints, and other articles.

Franklin: The Mary A. Proctor Collection includes more than sixty grooved axes, pestles, pipes, knives, and engraved stones.

Lakeport: The Abram L. Drake private collection has grinding stones used in that vicinity by the ancient Indians.

Rochester: The Harry L. Watson private collection has more than 2000 items from the Salmon Falls and Ossipee River areas.

The Weirs: The C. P. Wilcomb private collection has much material from the old Indian fishing village in this vicinity.

2. Exploration and Settlement to 1775

Exactly who were the first white people to see New Hampshire? We are not sure, but they were probably Scandinavian and Irish sailors and fishermen who sailed close to the New Hampshire coast and perhaps even landed there. Soon after Columbus found the New World in 1492, however, the English launched a search for the Northwest Passage. This meant a practical sailing route around the north end of the American continent to reach Asia. In 1496 a Venetian sea captain, Giovanni Caboto—or, as he was called in England, John Cabot—was commissioned by the then king of England, Henry VII, to pioneer the search for the "Northwest Passage." He made his first try in 1497 and his second effort in 1498. His little ship was named "Mathew," and his crew numbered eighteen men. Both voyages were frustrated by the steel-like hardness of the

Arctic ice. But Cabot's attempts gave the English a good claim to the northern parts of the new continent.

In the next century and a quarter many adventurous men sailed across the Atlantic Ocean to the New World, and some of them came to New Hampshire. For example, an English captain named Martin Pring visited the coasts of modern Maine and New Hampshire in 1603. In June of that year he sailed into the Great Bay and the Piscataqua River, and in his daily journal he wrote that he and his men on their ship, "Speedwell," saw

". . . very goodly groves and woods, replenished with tall Oakes, Beeches, Pine-trees, Firre-trees, Hasels, and Maples. We saw also sundry sorts of beasts, Deere, Bears, Wolves, Foxes, Lusernes, and Dogges with sharp noses."

In July, 1605, and again in September, 1606, the French explorer, Samuel de Champlain, sailed along the New Hampshire coast line. In 1614 the famous Captain John Smith, who had aided in the Virginia settlement in 1607, mapped the New England shore line all the way from Cape Cod to northern Maine. Upon returning to England, Captain Smith gave a copy of his map to the then Prince of Wales, who later became King Charles I. The latter was so pleased that he named the entire region New England, a title that has remained in use ever since. Captain Smith's map soon became well known and was consulted by every exploring and settling group for many years thereafter, including the Pilgrim Fathers in 1620.

The first permanent settlement within the bounds of present New Hampshire was begun on April 16, 1623. It happened in this way. A man named David Thomson secured a grant of land in the amount of 6000 acres from the Council for New England; his grant was dated November 15, 1622. In midwinter Thomson and his little group of followers sailed from Plymouth, England, on a ship named the "Jonathan." They landed on modern

Odiorne's Point in the town of Rye. The Thomson group built a trading post and some cabins at that place. Governor William Bradford of the Plymouth Rock colony in what is now Massachusetts twice mentioned the Thomson colony in his diary for 1623.

This Council for New England was a "joint-stock" company of forty prominent Englishmen which was chartered by King James I of England in 1620. Among its members were the Earl of Pembroke, the Earl of Salisbury, the Earl of Bath, and many other well-known people. You hear the names of these three men today in the names of three New Hampshire towns. The Council for New England was authorized to encourage English people to migrate to New England and to start settlements there. For many reasons at this time there were numerous men and women in England who wanted to leave and begin a new way of life in the New World. So the Council for New England was able to find many energetic and able people who became the first settlers and explorers for New Hampshire, as well as for other parts of New England.

On November 7, 1629, the Council granted to two men named John Mason and Fernando Gorges a large area of land between the Merrimack and the Piscataqua rivers extending upstream for sixty miles. This area, in the words of the 1629 charter, ". . . the said Captain John Mason, with the consent of the President and Council, intends to name NEW HAMPSHIRE." This was Mason's tribute to his home county of Hampshire in old England, and it has remained the name of the colony and state ever since. It is the only one of the present fifty American states which carries the exact name of one of the counties in old England. Another charter granted by the Council for New England to start settlements in New Hampshire was also given in 1629 to three brothers named Hilton, who started the town of Dover; and in 1631 nine other men including Mason and Gorges again were given a third charter covering a good deal of land in the seacoast region of New Hampshire. Of course, in those days the maps of the interior of New England were poor, and so the land bounds named by the charters are confusing and contradictory by modern standards.

There were four early towns of the new colony of New Hampshire. The first of these was Portsmouth, called "Strawberry Bank" until 1653. In 1631 a ship named the "Pied-Cowe" brought a load of settlers, together with supplies for them to Strawberry Bank. Portsmouth developed rapidly and was the chief town of New Hampshire for many years. Dover had some early settlers before 1629 but really began to grow after that year. In 1640 forty-two Dover men signed a document much like the Mayflower Compact of 1620. This New Hampshire paper is called "the Dover Combination." Exeter was begun in 1638 under the leadership of a noted minister named John Wheelwright. The original deed to the land on which the Wheelwright settlement was planted was secured from the Indians of that region and is still preserved in the library of the Phillips Exeter Academy. In late 1638 the fourth of the original little towns was started under the leadership of another minister named Stephen Bachiler. First called Winnacunnet, it was renamed Hampton in 1639.

These four New Hampshire towns had in all perhaps 1000 people in 1640. That year a great Civil War broke out in old England, and the four New Hampshire towns, seeking protection and safety, joined themselves to the much larger and more powerful neighboring colony of Massachusetts. This union lasted for almost exactly forty years. Many interesting things happened while little New Hampshire was a part of big Massachusetts. In 1642 a party of explorers first climbed to the top of Mount Washington. Ten years later, in 1652, another party went up the Merrimack River to its source and reached Lake Winnipesaukee at The Weirs. Here they chiseled their initials on a huge granite boulder by the riverbank, a boulder which is guarded and protected today by the state of New Hampshire. In 1673 Massachusetts granted a charter to a new town to be called Dunstable. It is today the city of Nashua. A fine map of New England was printed at Boston in 1677, which shows the

"White Hills" and the five towns of New Hampshire as they were then.

In 1679, however, the king of England, Charles II, decided that the time had come to reorganize New Hampshire as a separate colony once more. On September 18 of that year he ordained that on January 1, 1680, the New Hampshire people should again have their own government. He named John Cutt, a wealthy and respected merchant of Portsmouth, as the first governor. There were to be established also a Governor's Council, its members to be appointed by the king, and an assembly, to which each of the original four towns could send representatives. When the first elections to this assembly were held in 1680, Portsmouth had 71 voters; Dover 61; Hampton 57; and Exeter 20. In 1681 Governor Cutt fell ill and the council and assembly proclaimed Thursday, March 17, 1681, as a day ". . . of public fasting and prayer, to be kept by all the inhabitants." Such was the origin of New Hampshire's modern Fast Day, which is now legally observed each year in April.

New Settlements

From then on, settlements increased rapidly. By 1760 sixty-one towns had been chartered in New Hampshire. Between 1760 and 1775, when the War for Independence began, eighty-six new towns were started. Thus, when our forefathers began their struggle for independence from Great Britain in 1775, New Hampshire had grown to 147 towns with a population of 82,000 people. Many of these new towns took the names of famous Englishmen or women. Such towns as Chester and Hanover were derived from the royal family. Towns named for noted British soldiers or naval heroes included Amherst, Boscawen, Charlestown, Conway, Lee, Loudon, Peterborough, Temple, and Warren. Towns named for well-known Englishmen included Bedford, Bridgewater, Bristol, Chesterfield, Lempster, Meredith, Newport, Pembroke, Rochester, and Walpole. Other New Hampshire towns simply repeated the same names of towns of old England. These included Durham, Exeter, Plymouth, Portsmouth, and many others.

Among the most interesting people who came to New Hampshire during this period of rapid growth between 1680 and 1775 were the so-called Scotch Irish. Thousands of Scottish people had been transplanted to the northern part of Ireland, called Ulster, during the 1600s. In the early 1700s many of these people desired to leave Ireland. Some of them came to New England. In 1718 five shiploads of Scotch Irish landed in Boston. Most of them had come from Irish towns called Londonderry, Antrim, and Derry. In April, 1719, some of these new arrivals moved up into New Hampshire and began a new community. It was chartered as Londonderry in 1722. At first the Londonderry people assumed that their lands ran all the way to the Merrimack River, but later surveys ruled this interpretation invalid. So a new settlement called Derryfield was started along the banks of the Merrimack at Amoskeag Falls. This was the beginning of present-day New Hampshire's chief city, Manchester.

Londonderry is particularly interesting because it was a planned frontier community. Each house lot was laid out on West Running Brook and comprised about sixty acres. So successful was this method of settlement that it became the starting point for several other new towns, such as Windham, Litchfield, Antrim, Peterborough, and Acworth. The Scotch Irish were most able pioneers, early learning how to make log cabins and adapt themselves to the frontier. The Londonderry people were also expert at making fine linen, and they were the first in New England to raise the extremely important vegetable called the potato.

Soon after the Scotch Irish came into New Hampshire, an old quarrel flared up with Massachusetts. Ever since 1630 the leaders of that colony had claimed that the authority of Massachusetts extended up the valley of the Merrimack River as far north as The Weirs and thence all the way west to the Hudson River. If this were true, then the land in the present south-central and southwest portion of New Hampshire would belong to the Bay Colony. Of course, New Hampshire people did not accept this claim and a long legal battle ensued with lawyers on both sides arguing for their respective colony.

Finally, on March 5, 1740, King George II of England made his decision. The northern boundary of Massachusetts was set at the line which it follows today and all the area in controversy above that line was given to New Hampshire. This meant that Massachusetts lost twenty-eight towns in the valleys of the Merrimack and Connecticut rivers which it had chartered prior to 1740. Using their modern names, these included Bedford, Goffstown, Suncook, Bow, Concord, Penacook, Webster, Salisbury, New Boston, Dunbarton, Weare, Hopkinton, Warner, Bradford, Hinsdale, Westmoreland, Walpole, and Charlestown. In all, New Hampshire gained 3500 square miles by this decision of the king, including some of the most important parts of our present state. The new boundary line was surveyed in 1740, done over again in 1768, redone in 1789, and finally resurveyed with modern equipment late in the nineteenth century.

After 1740 another change came into the organization of New Hampshire. The king made it mandatory that New Hampshire should have a separate governor. Previous to this year, New Hampshire often had as governor the same man who was also governor of Massachusetts. Since this latter colony was much the bigger, the tendency was for the governor to spend most of his time in Boston and come to New Hampshire only rarely. But after 1740 the people of New Hampshire were pleased to have a governor entirely their own. The first was Benning Wentworth, who held the post from 1741 to 1766. He was followed by his nephew, John Wentworth, who took over from his uncle in 1767 and held the post until the War for Independence began in 1775. Both the Wentworths were able men who were well liked in New Hampshire, and whose interest in this area was very great.

Governor Benning Wentworth had great ambitions for New Hampshire. As he looked beyond the Connecticut River he saw the wilderness area which is the present state of Vermont. Beyond that was the English colony of New York. But Governor Wentworth insisted that the area between the Connecticut River and what is today the eastern boundary of New York was his to hold. In his commission of 1741 from the king, New Hampshire was defined as extending ". . . due West Cross the said river till it meets with our Other Governments." This certainly seemed to imply that New Hampshire extended to the New York line. According to the royal charter of 1664, this was supposed to run north and south on a line twenty miles east of the Hudson River. In 1749, therefore, Governor Wentworth chartered a town in what is now Vermont, which took the name of Bennington. By the time the great war with the French began in 1755—called the French and Indian War—Governor Wentworth had chartered sixteen towns in what is now Vermont, including Brattleboro, Putney, and Guilford. All this made the governor of New York very angry, and he claimed that the New Hampshire governor was completely wrong in issuing these town charters.

After the ending of the French and Indian War, Governor Wentworth continued to make more grants in Vermont. In the one year of 1760 he authorized sixty new towns west of the Connecticut River. By 1764 the number of Vermont towns for which he had issued charters had totaled 129. The governor of New York protested so strongly that in 1764 King George III made a ruling on the disputed boundary. By this royal order the Connecticut River was finally set as the western boundary of New Hampshire, and Governor Wentworth was told to issue no more town grants in Vermont. But what about those which he had already made? The arguments about this continued right up to the beginning of the war in 1775 and were the cause of all manner of friction between the people of New Hampshire and the people of New York.

It would be pleasant to think that this growth and development of New Hampshire had been accomplished without serious trouble with the Indians or with other white men. Unfortunately this was not the case. During the seventy years following 1689 there was a series of costly wars with the Indians and with the people of New France in the St. Lawrence Valley. Just as the English were developing their colonies along the Atlantic seacoast, so the nation called France was doing likewise to the north and west. New France, as it is called, was begun in 1604 and extended all the way from the area which today is the Canadian province of Nova Scotia to the mouth of the Mississippi River at New Orleans. Quebec, Montreal, Detroit, Duluth, St. Louis, and many other great cities of today were all started by remarkable French explorers and traders. These men roamed widely throughout the central part of our continent while the English were getting settled on the seaboard.

Most New Hampshire people cared nothing about this great expansion of French power into the valleys of Canada and the Great Lakes-Mississippi River area, as long as they could be left alone to develop their own farms and business. But this they could not do. Because of the quarrels between the king of England and the king of France, the people of Canada, then ruled by France, supported by most of the Indian tribes of the region, began to attack the people of New England in 1689. From then to 1760 there was little peace. Owing to its geographic location, New Hampshire was on the frontier between New England and New France, and almost every part of it saw fighting. We need not go into details of these wars. They were usually called by the name of the ruler who was then on the throne of England. Thus we have King William's War, 1689–1697; Queen Anne's War, 1701–1713; King George's War, 1744–1748; and finally the French and Indian War, 1755–1763.

The Indians by the time these wars began had come to fear

and dislike the white people of New England and New Hampshire. They saw that the number of whites was growing all the time. They kept pushing into the Indian hunting grounds, taking away the land, building towns, and driving the Indians away from their old homes. The French were not so likely to do this, for they were more inclined simply to be traders and trappers and did not settle down and build as many towns as did the English. Thus the French found that the Indians could be readily persuaded into becoming their allies. Therefore, on the French side the wars were usually fought partly with white soldiers, both Canadian and French, and partly with angry red men.

Raiding parties came down from Canada, using rivers and lakes, and suddenly burst upon the little farms and villages of New Hampshire. Before resistance could be mustered, they would rush back to Canada again. Sometimes they carried prisoners with them, expecting later to collect ransom money. In the first years of these wars, Durham, Dover, and other seacoast towns were burned, and the famous incident of Hannah Duston occurred.

In the spring of 1697 Haverhill, Massachusetts, was raided by a war party of Indians, and three women, including Mrs. Hannah Duston, were taken captive. The savages with their prisoners went north by the Merrimack River, and the second night out encamped on an island near the present town of Penacook. Recalling the story of Jael and Sisera from the Bible, Mrs. Duston arose in the night and killed all ten Indians in the party which had destroyed her week-old baby. She then with the aid of her companions scalped the dead men and returned to Massachusetts, collecting a bounty of £5 for each scalp. A monument on the island where this terrible episode occurred commemorates Hannah Duston.

By the 1740s there was a strong fort in western New Hampshire in what is now Charlestown. This was known as Old Number Four, because it was the most northerly of four frontier forts along the Connecticut River Valley. Old Number

Four was attacked by a large force of French and Indians in 1747, but successfully resisted. During this same period the towns of Penacook, Boscawen, and Concord were raided. One of the New Hampshire frontier leaders at this time was Colonel John Goffe. New Hampshire soldiers were also included in the English expedition that captured the great French fort of Louisburg on Cape Breton Island in 1745. A bell which the men brought back from Louisburg was presented to St. John's Episcopal Church in Portsmouth and is still a prized possession of that congregation.

The last and most bitter portion of the long struggle between England and France was the French and Indian War beginning in 1755. This was fought mostly in the Lake Champlain region. Among the New Hampshire soldiers who became noted in this conflict were two men named Robert Rogers and John Stark. Rogers was put in charge of a group of daring scouts called Rogers' Rangers. Stark was one of the leaders of this group. Some of their exciting adventures along the waterways extending into Canada from the present United States have been told by Kenneth Roberts in his novel, *Northwest Passage.* The decisive year of the war was 1759, for in that year the English and the colonists took the great French fort at Ticonderoga on Lake Champlain and the fortress of Quebec. In 1760 the final fighting of the war occurred when Montreal was captured. Then, at long last, the men could come home and New Hampshire knew peace again.

In the summer of 1760 Colonel John Goffe was ordered to take his regiment into the forests of Vermont and chop out a road all the way from Lake Champlain to the Connecticut River. This was the first highway across the present state of Vermont and represented the summer's labor of more than 500 men. The route of this original road in Vermont has been carefully traced by modern students, as it ran in a southeasterly direction from Crown Point on Lake Champlain to a terminus on the Connecticut River across from Charlestown. Indeed, there are one or two of the old granite milestones still in place, just where the soldiers set them in 1760.

Now that the wars were over, there was a rush for the new lands along the Connecticut River which the fighting men had seen during the war years, but which had never been safe for settlement until now. In the single year, 1761, Governor Wentworth granted charters for such new New Hampshire towns as Caanan, Enfield, Hanover, Lebanon, Lyme, Newport, Orford, Plainfield, and Rumney. In 1763 Cornish, Croydon, Haverhill, Lancaster, Plymouth, Sandwich, and Wentworth were among those chartered. In 1764 came Claremont, Franklin, and Unity; the next years saw the beginnings of Conway, Deerfield, and Tamworth.

In 1769, after years of discussion the colony of New Hampshire was divided into five counties. Each was named after an English nobleman. They bore the titles of Rockingham, Strafford, Hillsborough, Cheshire, and Grafton. These names are still found on the map of New Hampshire today, although they have been subdivided somewhat and five new counties have been formed.

By 1775 New Hampshire was a vigorous and growing colony, proud of its traditions and possessed of boundless energy with which to face the future.

3. *Living in Colonial New Hampshire*

The first settlers in New Hampshire lived in dwellings similar to those which they had used in England. Contrary to popular legend, they did not erect log cabins as soon as they landed on the shores of the New World, but built small houses of boards, roofed over with bark or perhaps rough shingles. They set up sawmills within a few years of landing, and the oldest house still standing in New Hampshire is built of boards sawed 300 years ago. This is the so-called Jackson House erected near modern Portsmouth in 1664. As soon as possible, the colonists began to make bricks from the abundant clays in the vicinity and used these for chimneys and in many instances for the exterior walls. As the New Hampshire pioneers moved into the hilly country to the west and north, they learned how to build log cabins and by the second century of the colony's existence, this type of house was appearing all along the frontier.

In their dwellings the early settlers of New Hampshire used all manner of wooden articles. Wooden bowls, plates, tableware, and spinning wheels were in common use. In the barns and fields wooden tools predominated. As time went on, the arts and skills of woodworking developed greatly. In the last half century before the War for Independence, fine furniture makers appeared in the colony of New Hampshire, making beautiful tables, chairs, cabinets, and dressers. Such pieces of furniture today are almost priceless and are eagerly sought after by wealthy collectors and by museums. In 1771, for instance, the town of Portsmouth alone exported more than 700 pieces of furniture. This was a greater volume of furniture export than the parallel figure for Philadelphia in the same year. (Philadelphia, of course, was many times larger than Portsmouth.) In 1762 New Hampshire had a famous clockmaker named Isaac Blaisdell, who lived in Chester and made clocks with brass works. Musical instruments like flutes, violins, and melodeons were also made by skilled workers in wood. Pewter makers, silversmiths, and pottery workers were found in many towns.

Craft skills were not confined to men. Women spun and wove cloth, especially wool and linen. Londonderry linen weavers in 1768 made more than 25,000 yards of fine linen cloth, and it was widely sold throughout colonial America. Beautiful needlework was done by many New Hampshire women. A quilt still remaining in the New Hampshire Historical Society at Concord was made by a young woman from Bow 200 years ago. It contains more than 42,000 separate pieces of fabric. Most clothing was homemade, including stockings and shoes. The housewife had to have many skills, and the art of sewing was one of the most important.

Along what might be called modern lines, colonial New Hampshire developed a good deal of ironmaking. So-called "bog iron" was found at many places in New England. In our area, it was found near Dover, Newmarket, Gilmanton, Kingston, and Bedford. The ironworkers dug this ore from the swamps and low areas and then smelted it over hot fires fed by charcoal. The charcoal was made from hard wood, which was "cooked" in turf-covered kilns until the charcoal was produced. It was estimated that a typical iron furnace would require at least 6000 cords of wood a year to make the necessary charcoal, so that many people found employment in cutting wood for this purpose.

Many of the workers of New Hampshire earned their living from forest products. The seacoast area was a center for shipbuilding. These shipyards constructed all kinds of craft, some of whose names sound queer today. These included shallops, pinnaces, sloops, pinks, ketches, brigs, snows, barks, schooners, smacks, and gundelows. Among the New Hampshire families who became prosperous because of this activity were the Langdons, the Wentworths, the Gilmans, the Swaseys, the Olivers, the Meserves, the Whipples, the Boyds, and the Warners. Just before 1775 the shipyards around Portsmouth alone were launching more than fifty vessels a year. Related to shipbuilding were such allied skills as ropemaking, wood carving, sailmaking, painting, caulking, blacksmithing, and the like.

Closely tied to the busy shipbuilding industry was the production of masts from the white pine forests. Even the British Navy came to depend upon these great trees from northern New England, principally New Hampshire and Maine. As early as 1634 the British Navy received a cargo of masts from Portsmouth, and for the next 140 years this trade was of vital significance to Great Britain. On the biggest ships of the Navy the mainmasts were sometimes forty yards long (120 feet) and forty inches through at the butt. Thanks to a plentiful supply of mast pines from New Hampshire, the British Navy came to be the world's greatest, and the "mast trade" became vital to British power and prestige. Even today many of the older towns have a street called "Mast Road." This marks the route by which the huge pines were dragged on sleds by ox teams in the winter to the river's edge. In the spring the great logs could be floated down to the ocean for shipment to Great Britain.

Another activity of men along the seacoast was fishing. This fishing business in New Hampshire, as elsewhere in New England, depended on the great abundance of codfish in the North Atlantic. These were caught in huge numbers, salted or smoked, and then sold in Europe. As early as 1671, for example, about 10,000 quintals of fish were exported from the one town of Portsmouth. A quintal was 112 pounds. In addition to the cod, New Hampshire fishermen caught such ocean creatures as clams, lobsters, pollack, herring, and many other varieties. Salt was made by evaporating sea water. It was from fishermen like these that the American Navy recruited its first sailors after 1775, and fishermen like these a few years later were to take the whaling ships into the most remote parts of the world in chase of the largest animals which have ever existed.

Without doubt, the majority of New Hampshire people in the colonial period made their living off the land. These hard-working men and women, unassisted by any power machinery, cut the trees, pulled out the stones, and planted the hard-won fields to crops. Wheat and corn were widely raised, as were such vegetables as beans, peas, pumpkins, squashes, root crops like beets and carrots, and cabbage. Tomatoes were not known in colonial New Hampshire, nor were such vegetables as broccoli or head lettuce. The first potatoes grown in all New England were introduced into New Hampshire at Derry shortly after 1719 and rapidly became a staple of diet. Numerous "grist mills" along the rapidly flowing streams and rivers ground wheat and corn into flour and corn meal, and these also were basic food items.

The principal fruit of colonial New Hampshire was apples. The early settlers brought with them from the old country either seeds or cuttings and grew such apples as Russets, Pippins, and Sweetings. After 1740 the Baldwin apple was introduced into New Hampshire from Massachusetts and the Newton apple from Long Island. From these apples New

Hampshire people made cider and vinegar, each useful in its way. Although they knew nothing about the importance of Vitamin C in their diet, our forefathers learned by experience that "an apple a day keeps the doctor away," and used this fruit in many ways. They also had plums, pears, peaches, and some kinds of grapes. Citrus fruits were almost unheard of in colonial days. Only occasionally a ship captain would bring in lemons and oranges, and a few people along the seacoast had the pleasure of tasting these rare fruits. The people well knew the delicious taste of maple sirup and maple sugar, and in many homes these were the only sweetenings used.

Most farmers, of course, in addition to grain and vegetable crops, raised cattle, horses, sheep, and pigs. These animals of colonial times were much smaller than the farm stock we know today. The science of animal husbandry was just beginning to be understood in Europe by 1775, and the first experiments in developing better breeds were under way. Yet from the farm animals of colonial New Hampshire came milk, butter and cheese, leather, and meat. Meat was preserved largely by smoking it, as in the case of ham and bacon, or salting it as in the case of pork and beef. The leather made shoes and some garments. The wool from the sheep was spun into yarn and made into clothing. From the great forests came a plentiful supply of wild game and some varieties of food now no longer available, such as chestnuts. Country people knew how to catch and preserve the abundant fish of the lakes and rivers. They had, also, one source of food supply now gone forever, the enormous flocks of passenger pigeons whose flights frequently darkened the sky. Migratory birds like geese and ducks were far more abundant then than they are today.

There were no legally incorporated cities in colonial New Hampshire; even the largest settlement, Portsmouth, was still a town. Yet in those towns there were the beginnings of many professional occupations found in urban areas today. For example, New Hampshire had its first newspaper when a printer named David Towle began publishing his weekly *New*

Hampshire Gazette in 1756. A few lawyers lived in Portsmouth and elsewhere in the older parts of New Hampshire. Medical care, as in other places in colonial America, was in the hands of physicians who, for the most part, had been trained in England or in Scotland. There was no institution like a hospital, as we understand that term. The two best-known medical men in the colony were Dr. Matthew Thornton of Londonderry and Dr. Josiah Bartlett of Kingston. Both were notable for their public service as well as for their medical skills. They were pioneers in the use of new treatments.

The mass of the people, in ordinary illnesses, relied on home remedies. There was a widespread knowledge of and use of herbs. Inoculation for smallpox was introduced into New Hampshire about 1730. While not vaccination in the modern sense, this treatment provided a kind of protection against the ravages of that disease. Other much dreaded forms of sickness were typhus, dysentery, typhoid fever, pneumonia, diphtheria, and scurvy. Men like Dr. Bartlett experimented with the use of quinine to mitigate the fevers of malarial ailments. But despite the simpler conditions of life then and the greater exposure to fresh air and sunshine, the incidence of sickness was high and the death rate much higher than today.

In the early days New Hampshire had no real roads, only trails usable by horseback riders or by travelers on foot. The first adequate road, although primitive by present-day standards, was built across the seacoast region to connect Portsmouth with Boston. By 1761 this had been improved so that on a twice-a-week basis a stagecoach began to operate across the colony between these two settled areas. In the winter stage travel was slow and uncertain. When they went by stage, travelers were always advised to carry some food with them, preferably a pot of baked beans. From this custom arose the famous jingle:

> *Bean porridge hot; bean porridge cold;*
> *Bean porridge in the pot, nine days old.*

Extended road building in New Hampshire had to await the conclusion of the last war with the French. In 1763 plans were made to construct a highway from Dover to Haverhill on the Upper Connecticut. This was actually surveyed in 1768, but it was not finished until after the War for Independence. In 1770 a road from Boscawen to Charlestown was begun. In 1771 Crawford Notch was first discovered by white men, and a road was soon projected through this mountain gorge. In 1771, also, the so-called "College Highway," from Wolfeborough to Hanover by way of Plymouth, was started. Mail service between New Hampshire and Boston was initiated as early as 1697. Postal rates then were much higher than they are today and varied in accordance with the distance the letter was to travel.

As better roads developed, so did the necessity of finding a satisfactory way to get across the rivers and streams. In the beginning, travelers had to cross at some shallow place in the river called a "ford." Gradually, however, skills in bridge-making improved. These brought about that structure famous in New England known as the covered bridge. This was not a new invention, for the Chinese had used covered bridges long before the birth of Christ, and in European countries like Switzerland even today there are covered bridges which were built before Columbus discovered America. It is not possible to state with assurance just where the first covered bridge was erected in New Hampshire, but it was probably in the coastal area. By 1785 enough skill in such building had been developed so that a long covered bridge was put across the Connecticut River in the town of Walpole. Its span was 365 feet, with the floor fifty feet above the surface of the water. Even by modern standards this was a large bridge.

It is clear that the colonists of New Hampshire were energetic and successful in material things. They displayed the same characteristics in other aspects of life. When the colony began in the 1600s, the Congregational Church, as we call it today, was the predominant one. When the Scotch Irish arrived in 1719, they brought with them the Presbyterian faith. Other communions to appear in the early days included the Quakers, the Baptists, and the Episcopalians. In 1775 there were eighty-four Congregational churches in New Hampshire; fifteen Presbyterian; eleven Baptist; two Quaker; and two Episcopalian. There were no Roman Catholic or Greek Catholic churches in the colony, nor were there any Jewish synagogues. Each town by tax money supported the church favored by the majority of the voters at town meeting, and the minister was a paid servant of the town. Some of these New Hampshire colonial ministers were famous for their long pastorates. Ebenezer Hall was at Mason for fifty-eight years; Joseph Adams preached at Newington for sixty-eight years; and Laban Ainsworth was at Jaffrey for seventy-six years, observing his one-hundredth birthday while still serving as minister! All three were Congregational clergymen. Ministers of this faith held the majority of pastorates in colonial New Hampshire.

In the language of our forefathers the word "church" meant an association of people, not a building. The building in which these people worshiped was called the "meetinghouse." The meetinghouse was the chief public building of the town and was used by the citizens for many purposes other than religious services. As Mrs. Eva Speare says in her little book, *Colonial Meeting-Houses in New Hampshire*[1]:

The importance of the meeting-house in the development of the infant townships can not be overestimated. Here was the only building where the entire population could be accommodated; here was the seat of government, both sacred and secular, where the laws of God were taught on Sunday, and the laws of men were framed at monthly, or, if necessity demanded, at weekly town meetings. Within these walls the taxes were levied, schools established, highways and bridges planned, and the general welfare promoted. . . . The forum of free speech was the New England meeting-house.

[1] *See Bibliography referring to Chapter 3.*

The oldest such building still standing in New Hampshire is in Newington. It was opened in 1713. About thirty other meetinghouses dating back to a time before 1775 are still standing.

Many of these old meetinghouses were simple and unpretentious structures, resembling, in fact, a barn. One of them which has attracted much attention in our day is in the town of Danville. Here the main entrance into the meetinghouse was in the middle of the long exterior wall. Around three sides of the interior were balconies, with box pews and gates to them. A high pulpit was placed exactly opposite the main door. Above the high pulpit was a sounding board so that the minister's voice could better be heard. On the main floor the box pews had bench-like seats on all four sides. In the beginning there was no heating, and in cold weather the attendants at worship services or other gatherings had to bring foot warmers with them. Such a building would have no steeple, no bell, and no exterior or interior decorations.

Colonial New Hampshire had laws which made elementary education obligatory for children in all towns. The "dame schools" provided the beginnings of reading and writing for the youngest children; "3-R" schools the rudiments of elementary education; and "Latin Grammar Schools" more advanced secondary education. Very few boys and girls went beyond the "3-R" schools. This was the era of the one-room little red schoolhouse (some of which still exist in New Hampshire as well as in other states) where children of all grades and ages recited in small classes.

Teachers were frequently men, and discipline was severe. A basic textbook was the *New England Primer,* which originally appeared in Boston in 1690. Happily, colonial children did have some lighter reading, including "The House that Jack Built," which was known and recited in our schools as early as 1740. By 1775, the first appearance of *Mother Goose* was noted in New Hampshire.

In 1769 the Reverend Eleazer Wheelock of Lebanon, Connecticut, a graduate of Yale College in the class of 1733, obtained from Governor Wentworth a charter to establish a college in New Hampshire ". . . for the education & instruction of Youth of the Indian tribes . . . and also of English Youth and any others." The settlers of the little town of Hanover on the Upper Connecticut River, chartered in 1761, offered Wheelock a tract of 3000 acres of land, plus other benefits, if he would locate his new college in their community. Wheelock gratefully accepted this proposition and in 1770 came to Hanover to build the first structure of his institution. He named it Dartmouth after the Earl of Dartmouth in England, a friend who had given a considerable sum of money to get the college started. In 1771 the first class of four students enrolled at Dartmouth, and that famous institution was in operation. It was the ninth and last college to be started in the thirteen colonies before the outbreak of the War for Independence in 1775.

Music in New Hampshire in colonial times was principally heard in church. The *Bay Psalm Book,* the first volume ever published in British North America, appeared in Boston in 1640 and was used by most churches in New Hampshire. There were no music notes in the book, simply the words. The singers had to know the tunes or else not sing at all. These early hymns used many of the words of the Psalms in the Bible. It was not until late in colonial times that the idea of original hymns was acceptable to most churches. Perhaps the two best-liked hymns of this nature were "O God, Our Help in Ages Past," by Isaac Watts, and "Jesus, Lover of My Soul," by John Wesley. Both these men were English writers, but Wesley visited some of the thirteen colonies and knew their people well.

As for sports and recreation, New Hampshire people enjoyed horse racing, hunting, fishing, lacrosse, wrestling, and a type of primitive baseball. Some girls had dolls, and some boys were permitted to have toys of various kinds. There were no stage plays or theater performances in New Hampshire before 1775. In 1762 a number of people in Portsmouth petitioned the governor to let them start a theater. But more people petitioned him not to permit it. The governor yielded to the wishes of the majority. Smoking and the use of liquor were widespread, but not so evident in public as today. Those who overindulged in strong drink or other bad habits were often put in the "stocks" on the village common or sometimes placed in the "ducking stool" and immersed in the town pond.

Political leadership in New Hampshire was in the hands of a governor appointed by the king in London, his council, and an assembly elected by the people themselves. Between 1680 and 1775 there were nineteen governors, of whom the best known were Joseph Dudley, 1701–1715; Benning Wentworth, 1741–1766; and John Wentworth, 1767–1775. The council consisted usually of nine men appointed by the governor. The assembly was elected by the adult male voters of the colony. By the end of the colonial period the majority of men over twenty-one years of age were able to vote. Between 1680 and 1775 there were fifty-three elected assemblies in New Hampshire. In the last assembly before the War for Independence there were thirty-four members, selected from thirty-four towns. The bigger places usually had more than one representative, while the smaller towns "doubled up" on their delegates. The assembly clearly represented the mass of the people, while the council and the governor just as clearly represented the wealthier and more socially prominent element in the community.

The institution of the town meeting, very like that which we know today, was found in the earliest history of New Hampshire. The selectmen were the chief officers of the town and were elected at the annual meeting. Next to the selectmen in importance were the town clerk, the tax collector, and the treasurer. Of course there was a moderator for the meeting, and there were constables to enforce the laws. Many town offices of those days are not found in modern communities: these now outworn titles would include pound-keeper, cask-gauger, hog-reeve, tythingman, and fence-viewer. But the problems debated in town meetings 200 or more years ago were basically the same as those discussed in town meeting today: taxes, roads and highways, school costs, law enforcement, honesty in business, and fire prevention.

Such was the life of the people in colonial New Hampshire in 1775 when the War for Independence began.

4. *Helping to Win Independence and Build a New Nation*

The French and Indian War came to an end with the signing of the Treaty of Paris on February 10, 1763. There ensued a most interesting postwar period of twelve years in New Hampshire and in the other colonies. On the one hand, the people rejoiced at the return of peace and the possibility of living a normal life once more. As already noted, the Governors Wentworth granted scores of town charters in the years after 1763. The valley of the Connecticut River and the hill country north and west of the Merrimack River had a great influx of new settlers. In 1767 New Hampshire took its first regular census, and a population of 52,700 was recorded. Just eight years later, as the War for Independence was about to begin, the final colonial census showed 82,000 people in New Hampshire. During these years, new roads were built, Dartmouth College was founded, and much more that was constructive and peaceful began.

On the other hand, the twelve years between 1763 and 1775 were a period of extreme tension between the British government in London and its American colonies, including New Hampshire. It proved to be impossible to restore the old relationship that had once existed between mother country and colonists, and friction rather than harmony was the order of the day. In the bitter struggle and argument that followed, Americans fell into three groups: the patriots, who asserted their rights and even began to dream of independence; the Tories, who longed for the old ways and thought loyalty to Great Britain was their chief duty; and the in-between group which was confused and hardly knew what to think. As time went on, the majority of people in New Hampshire came more and more to belong to the first group. But there were some who insisted on being Tories, and others who hoped to "sit on the fence" until the arguments were over. Governor Wentworth, of course, was the leader of the Tories.

What were the arguments that grew so bitter between Great Britain and her thirteen colonies? Four of them were of vital importance to the growing communities. In the first place, there was a strong difference of opinion over taxation. The British government had gone deeply into debt in its effort to win the French and Indian War, and Parliament felt that the colonists should help pay this debt. Such a levy of taxes the patriots resisted, claiming that the British Parliament had no right to place financial burdens on them without their own consent. Secondly, the better to protect North America, in 1763 the British decided to maintain a standing army of regular troops in the colonies; 10,000 of them were planned for garrison duty here. This policy also the Americans resented, insisting that they were perfectly able to defend themselves. Thirdly, the British government after 1763 was determined to keep the colonists from crossing the Appalachian Mountains.

The whole area of the Ohio and Mississippi Valley which the British then owned they planned to leave in the possession of the Indians. This policy many colonists emphatically disliked. Finally, there was some thought in London about setting up the Episcopal Church as the official church in all the colonies. This possibility greatly angered colonists of other denominations.

In addition to these and similar grievances which rapidly grew between 1763 and 1775, there was another feeling harder to define, but none the less important. This was a conviction which was developing in all the colonies from New Hampshire to Georgia, the feeling that the people living in them were "Americans." In other words, as we have seen in so many nations in today's world, the idea of nationalism was appearing. Like their friends in other colonies, New Hampshire folk were coming to think of themselves as free people owing few, if any, duties to Great Britain. They no longer feared invasion from Canada; they no longer were worried about the Indians; they no longer were dependent on the mother country. On the contrary, they were proud of their own leaders and what they had done in the French and Indian War. Veterans who had fought for years in the struggle with France now formed the core of the minutemen, as the trained militia of New Hampshire was called. Officers like John Stark were their heroes. And many of these officers did not like the British and were willing to oppose them. They were to become the leaders of open resistance in 1775.

Therefore, in 1765, when Parliament passed the Stamp Act levying a tax on the American colonies, New Hampshire experienced a surge of anger. On November 22 that year the New Hampshire Assembly unanimously passed a resolution disapproving the Stamp Act. In 1767, when Parliament put through the so-called Townshend Acts—named for the British government leader who proposed them—New Hampshire was again aroused. In 1773 Parliament passed the ill-starred Tea Act, levying a tax on this popular beverage. New Hampshire public opinion was firmly against this law; it applauded the Boston Tea Party on December 16, 1773; and it almost had a similar tea party of its own at Portsmouth the next spring. As Meshech Weare put it:

> Rouse every generous thoughtful mind,
> The rising danger flee,
> If you would lasting freedom find
> Now then abandon tea.

In 1773 the New Hampshire Assembly showed its spirit by appointing seven of its members to serve as a "Standing Committee of Correspondence and Inquiry." This committee was charged with the duty of keeping in touch with like-minded committees in the other twelve colonies.

Beginnings of Forceful Resistance

In 1774 the British government sought to punish Massachusetts for its actions in the Boston Tea Party the previous year. But the penalties which Great Britain laid upon Massachusetts simply aroused more indignation against Great Britain in other colonies, particularly in New Hampshire. In September, 1774, a great protest meeting against British actions was called in Philadelphia. This was styled the First Continental Congress. To it from New Hampshire went Nathaniel Folsom of Exeter and John Sullivan of Durham. Three months later, in December, 1774, a Massachusetts messenger named Paul Revere came into Portsmouth with alarming news of British plans to strengthen their forces in New England. On the night of December 15 an armed group of New Hampshire men, led by Thomas Pickering and John Langdon of Portsmouth, marched to old Fort William and Mary, a British strongpoint in New Castle. They entered the fort and confiscated a hundred barrels of gunpowder. The next day more equipment and more supplies were taken from the fort. Governor Wentworth was extremely angry at this seizure of British military equipment, but he could do nothing against the aroused public opinion of the majority of the people. This action of New Hampshire men in December, 1774, was the first armed resistance to Great Britain in the colonies.

Now the tides of rebellion began to run even faster. On April 14, 1775, General Gage, the British commander in chief in Boston, received secret instructions from his government in London. He was ordered to arrest the leaders of the patriot group in New England and to confiscate all military supplies which they had collected. Just four nights later Gage put his orders into effect. He dispatched 700 British soldiers to two Massachusetts towns named Lexington and Concord, where he believed patriots were hiding and where he thought supplies had been gathered. In the morning and throughout the day of April 19, fighting took place in both towns; the British were worsted by the minutemen and retreated to Boston. As soon as the American victory was known, fast horsemen hurried the news of what had happened to all parts of the colonies. The exciting news had reached New Hampshire by the morning of April 20. Soon minutemen began to assemble on village greens and shortly thereafter started south to the aid of Massachusetts.

From Epsom, Captain Andrew McClary led thirty-four men, who marched seventy miles to Cambridge within twenty-four hours. From Epping, Dr. Henry Dearborn took 100 men to Medford, sixty miles in a little over twelve hours. From Rindge, Captain Nathan Hale took fifty-four men to Cambridge. From Keene, Captain Isaac Wyman marched twenty-nine men to Lexington, arriving there two days later. From Exeter, Captain James Hackett took 108 men to Cambridge. Perhaps best known of all, Captain John Stark on April 21 took numerous followers from Amoskeag Falls to Lexington. On the twenty-second he received a colonel's commission from Massachusetts and assumed command of all New Hampshire minutemen within the Bay Colony. By the end of the month these numbered more than 2000.

Thus began New Hampshire's military effort to assist in the American War for Independence. It never ceased until the end of the struggle. While it is impossible today to state exactly how many different men from New Hampshire served in the American armies during the eight years from 1775–1783—many men enlisted for more than one term, the usual enlistment at the beginning being for one year only—it is probable that the total exceeded 5000. Perhaps half of these served as minutemen. The remainder enlisted in the regular Continental Army regiments which were authorized by Congress. New Hampsire had three such regiments during the war. Of their services to the patriot cause, Richard F. Upton has written[2]:

They helped repulse the British at Bunker Hill. They marched with Sullivan's ill-fated Canadian expedition, and died like flies from smallpox on the retreat. They composed the right wing at Trenton and participated in the rapid counter march to "outfox" Cornwallis at Princeton. They followed Arnold in his headlong charge at Saratoga. They shivered and starved at Valley Forge. They counter-attacked savagely at Monmouth. They devastated the country of the Six Nations. They were present at the surrender at Yorktown. They watched the British finally evacuate New York. The First New Hampshire Regiment had served continuously for a period of eight years and eight months—probably the longest service record of any Revolutionary regiment.

Two New Hampshire men rose to the rank of major general in the American armies: John Sullivan of Durham and John Stark of Amoskeag Falls. Other well-known New Hampshire officers not already mentioned included Enoch Poor of Exeter, Timothy Bedel of Bath, James Reed of Fitzwilliam, Benjamin Whitcomb of Westmoreland, and Alexander Scammell of Durham. There was no actual fighting in New Hampshire during the war; indeed this was the only state of the thirteen where there was no bloodshed. But New Hampshire officers and men

2 *See Bibliography referring to Chapter 4.*

participated in every major encounter during the long struggle.

One of the most significant years of the war, insofar as New Hampshire was concerned, was 1777. In that year General Stark was placed in command of 1400 New Hampshire minutemen and went to Vermont to help stop the British troops under General Burgoyne, coming down from Canada. At the important Battle of Bennington in mid-August, Stark and his soldiers were successful in defeating the invading forces. In connection with this campaign, Speaker John Langdon of the New Hampshire House of Representatives in a stirring address pledged all his possessions to help the patriot cause, saying:

They are at the service of the State. If we succeed in defending our firesides and our homes, I may be remunerated. If we do not, the property will be of no value to me.

Later this same year Captain John Paul Jones took command of the U.S.S. "Ranger," built at Portsmouth, and sailed out on the high seas to fight the British. His was the first naval ship ever to fly the present American flag, the Stars and Stripes, which had been authorized by Congress in June, 1777.

THE HOME FRONT, 1775–1784

It was not enough, of course, to fight on land and on sea. New Hampshire had also to undertake many activities on the home front. For example, the people had to reorganize their political structure and turn the old colony into the new state of New Hampshire. In January, 1776, New Hampshire became the first of the thirteen states to adopt a formal constitution, destined to last until 1784. Upton describes it as follows[3]:

Under this Constitution, all the powers of government were held by a bicameral legislature, consisting of a house of representatives and a council. There was no governor or chief executive as such, nor was there a judicial department. These gaps were filled by

3 *See Bibliography referring to Chapter 4.*

legislation. The pre-existing system of courts and the pre-existing code of laws were re-established so far as consistent with the status of independence. A Committee of Safety was established and appointed by the legislature to serve as the executive power. This committee varied in size from eight to twelve members.

Meshech Weare was chosen president of the council or upper house of legislature and served in this capacity throughout the Revolution. He was elected chairman of the Committee of Safety and served in this capacity throughout the Revolution. He was appointed Chief Justice of the Superior Court, then the highest state court, and served in this position from 1776 to 1782, when he resigned at age 69 due to the pressure of his other duties and failing health. This was a remarkable example of public trust in one man. It is as if today the same man held at one time the offices of governor, president of the senate and chief justice of the supreme court. His contemporaries record that he possessed a well balanced temperament and excellent self-control. He was also noted for his fairness, shrewdness and honesty. He left office considerably poorer than when he entered it, indicating that, because of his devotion to the public service, he probably neglected his private affairs.

The Committee of Safety over which Meshech Weare presided was a most interesting revolutionary institution. It operated at state level and also locally through a network of committees of safety in each of the towns. During recesses of the legislature, the Committee was practically a law unto itself with power "to take under their consideration all matters in which the welfare of the province, in the security of their rights, shall be concerned, except the appointment of field officers, and to take utmost care that the Public sustain no damage." This was certainly a broad grant of power, and it was broadly interpreted in practice.

The New Hampshire Declaration of Independence was signed on June 15, 1776, about three weeks before the national Declaration of Independence was proclaimed in Philadelphia. Our state was represented by three names on this famous national document: Josiah Bartlett, Matthew Thornton, and William Whipple. Between 1775 and 1783 New Hampshire sent fourteen different men to the Continental Congress, which tried to govern the whole nation, mostly holding its sessions in Philadelphia. This body supervised the conduct of the war, conducted negotiations with foreign countries, and sought to raise armies and navies large enough to bring about victory. Among other accomplishments, it wrote the first national constitution for the United States, the Articles of Confederation, adopted in 1781.

A difficult problem was how to deal with those people who preferred the Tory side of the war, that is those who remained loyal to Great Britain. While these were not numerous in New Hampshire, they included a number of wealthy and prominent citizens in the new state. On April 12, 1776, the Committee of Safety in New Hampshire prepared a pledge of allegiance to the patriot cause which was called "the Association Test." It was to be administered by the authorities in each town to every adult male over twenty-one years of age. More than 9000 men in New Hampshire were confronted with the test; 8567 signed it without reservations; 781 refused to sign. Those who refused were immediately subject to criticism and in some cases punishment. More than a hundred families left New Hampshire, leaving their property behind them. This property was then taken over by the state government and sold to raise money for the war effort.

Another and perhaps more difficult problem on the home front was the attitude of a number of the towns in the western and northern portions of the state. Many of these had been chiefly settled by people from Connecticut and lay along the banks of the river of the same name. They had not been properly represented either in the colonial assembly or in the new state legislature. Their people were closely related by ties of acquaintance and business with the citizens of similar towns on the west or Vermont side of the river. It was therefore proposed that sixteen of these northern and western New Hampshire towns join with the new state of Vermont, organized in 1777. On July 11, 1778, this was done. Sixteen New Hampshire communities—including Cornish, Lebanon, Hanover, Lyme,

Orford, and others—seceded from New Hampshire and became a part of Vermont. But later that year the sixteen towns were released from their pledges to stay with Vermont and left free to choose their own future. After three years of confusion, in 1781 the same sixteen towns, plus twenty additional New Hampshire communities, again joined with Vermont. But in 1782 this agreement also was canceled, and the thirty-six towns permanently came back to New Hampshire again.

Other aspects of life in our state during the conflict may be mentioned briefly. The Committee of Safety tried to set price controls during the war, seeking to protect the consumer against rapidly rising price levels. But this experiment did not succeed. Much paper money was printed, and it lost most of its value before the war was over. A considerable number of new towns were started during the war, and the population of the state grew slowly. One of these new towns was Washington. Incorporated under that name on December 13, 1776, it was the first place in the nation to take the name of the man who was already being called the "Father of His Country." There was renewed interest in religion; such denominations as the Freewill Baptists, the Methodists, and the Universalists appeared in the state.

In 1784 the people established another constitution to take the place of the original one prepared in 1776. The new document was modeled closely upon the Massachusetts constitution of 1780, and much of it is still in effect today. Under it the chief executive was styled the President. During the next few years four men, all famous during the War for Independence, were elected to this post: Meshech Weare, John Langdon, John Sullivan, and Josiah Bartlett. The constitution was revised again in 1792, when the title of the chief officer of the state was changed to governor. In 1784 the state seal was designed and adopted by the legislature. Most of the time during these early years, the legislature held its sessions in Concord, but occasionally it met in Exeter, Portsmouth, Hopkinton, and Charlestown. The treaty of peace that ended the war was approved by Congress in 1784, and New Hampshire settled down to what people hoped would be a season of peace and prosperity.

Helping to Build the New Nation

But within a few years more problems appeared. The Articles of Confederation were not proving to be satisfactory as a basis of national government. In 1787 an important convention was called at Philadelphia to prepare a new and improved constitution for the United States. New Hampshire sent John Langdon and Nicholas Gilman as its delegates to this important meeting. They did not reach Philadelphia until late July, but remained there and signed the great document on September 17. It was agreed that the constitution would go into effect when nine of the thirteen states had approved it.

By the next summer eight states had given their approval, but the ninth had not expressed itself. At this juncture, a state convention was called to meet in Concord in June, to consider whether or not New Hampshire would approve the document, thus putting it into effect. After three days of debate, on June 21, 1788, the New Hampshire convention by a vote of fifty-four to forty-seven approved the new U.S. Constitution. Fast horsemen carried the important news to all parts of the nation, and friends of the United States rejoiced that it now had a strong central government. That fall the voters throughout the nation chose their first President, George Washington, and elected the the first Congress. The capital city for the nation was temporarily to be New York, and there on April 30, 1789, the new President took his oath of office. New Hampshire was pleased that one of its U.S. senators, John Langdon, was named the first president pro tempore of the Senate.

Shortly after Congress adjourned in that autumn of 1789, President Washington decided to visit New England. Traveling by stagecoach, he and his party reached New Hampshire on the last day of October. With great pomp and ceremony the President of the United States was escorted to Portsmouth, where he was enthusiastically welcomed by a large crowd. They sang an original hymn in his honor to the same tune that we now use in "America." One verse went as follows:

> Long may thy Trumpet, Fame,
> Let echo waft the Name
> Of WASHINGTON
> O'er all the world around
> Far as earth's utmost bound,
> Thy equal is not found,
> Columbia's Son.

The distinguished guests stayed in Portsmouth for three full days and did not leave until November 4.

In the busy years following the close of the War for Independence, many new developments not connected with government or politics took place in New Hampshire. For example, the Reverend Jeremy Belknap, pastor of the Congregational Church in Dover from 1766 to 1786, wrote and published the first adequate history of New Hampshire. It set a fashion which writers in other states were quick to imitate. In 1784 an exploring party under the leadership of Manasseh Cutler carefully studied and named the great peak of the White Mountains after George Washington. On February 16, 1791, the New Hampshire Medical Society was formed with nineteen doctors as original members. First president of the new group was Dr. Josiah Bartlett. Five new academies were started in the state, seeking to do work similar to that begun in 1783 at Phillips Exeter. In 1792 the legislature incorporated the New Hampshire Bank in Portsmouth, the sixth bank in the entire United States. Between 1780 and 1789 a boy named Sam Wilson lived on a farm near Mason. After he passed his twenty-first birthday, young Wilson moved to Troy, New York. There he engaged in the meat-packing business, supplying beef to the army. Soldiers who knew Wilson personally referred to their beef as "Uncle Sam's." As the initials "U.S." were stamped on the barrels from which it came, "Uncle Sam" and "U.S." came to be synonymous, and Sam Wilson personified the government itself. Thus he became the original of "Uncle Sam," the nickname for our country today.

5. The Young State:
Old Patterns Begin to Change

More than half the people in New Hampshire were classified as rural until the United States census of 1910. For that reason its public affairs were dominated by the political party that most appealed to the farmers and country people. For the first half of the nineteenth century this meant the followers of Thomas Jefferson and Andrew Jackson, the party known today as Democratic.

As the first Democratic President in the White House, Jefferson organized and sent to the Pacific Coast a great exploring expedition led by the noted officers, Lewis and Clark. One of the members of this remarkable group was Sergeant John

Ordway of Bow, New Hampshire. His journal of this expedition, which has been preserved, was used to supplement the record of Lewis and Clark and is the sole record of the exploration of the headwaters of the Missouri River undertaken by Clark with Ordway. Another noted early Democratic President was James Monroe. In July, 1817, President Monroe came to New Hampshire for a visit and was granted an honorary degree by Dartmouth College. In June, 1825, the famous Marquis de Lafayette from France visited New Hampshire and was greeted at Concord by over 200 veterans of the War for Independence. In June, 1833, President Andrew Jackson, at the invitation of the New Hampshire Legislature, visited our state. Fourteen years later, President James K. Polk became the fourth chief executive to visit New Hampshire while in office.

On the thirty-second anniversary of the Battle of Bennington, a great meeting was held in the Vermont town of that name where General John Stark had led the Americans to victory in 1777. The old general, then living in retirement in Derryfield (now Manchester), was asked to attend the reunion. He could not make the long trip, but he sent the gathering a message which included the famous words, "Live Free or Die." It is this expression of John Stark's which has now become the official motto of New Hampshire. Although General Stark heartily supported the War of 1812 against Great Britain a few years later, many New Hampshire people were not particularly interested in the conflict and welcomed the return of peace once more in 1815. Governor of New Hampshire when the War of 1812 began was William Plumer, one of the most interesting men who ever occupied the post.

In 1816 Governor Plumer and the New Hampshire Legislature started action which was to have an important outcome. This was nothing less than an effort by state law to turn Dartmouth College into a public university. The leaders of the college denied that the state had any such right and insisted that the charter which had been granted by the king to that institution in 1769 made Dartmouth a private college forever.

49

The long argument which resulted had to be settled by the Supreme Court of the United States in a decision announced on February 2, 1819. Attorney for the college was a rising young lawyer who had been born in Salisbury, New Hampshire, in 1782. His name was Daniel Webster. This Dartmouth College Case, brilliantly argued by Webster, made him a national figure and has become a milestone in American history. A friend wrote to the president of Dartmouth:

> I would have an inscription over the door of your building, "Founded by Eleazar Wheelock, Refounded by Daniel Webster!"

The population of New Hampshire was growing steadily during these years. In 1820 it numbered over 244,000; ten years later it was more than 269,000; while by 1860 it had risen to 326,000. New counties were created to handle the increasing public business: Coos in 1803; Merrimack in 1823; Sullivan in 1827; Belknap and Carroll in 1840. This brought the total of counties to ten, the same number as at present. In 1823 the New Hampshire Historical Society was formed in Concord, dedicated to the preservation and study of New Hampshire history. Governor Plumer—who served four different terms of one year each—in 1813 was responsible for the building of the first state prison in New Hampshire; in 1819 he pushed through to completion the building which is still the central portion of our state capitol today. In 1820 Plumer prevented the election of President Monroe from being unanimous by casting his vote as a presidential elector against Monroe. So Washington's record has never been equaled: he was the only man ever *unanimously* elected President of the United States.

After the War of 1812 was over, New Hampshire pioneers began to move into the northernmost parts of the state. Exactly where the boundary was between the United States and Canada remained somewhat uncertain until 1842, when it was finally settled by treaty. In the meantime, an area called the Indian Stream, containing about 100,000 acres of wild forest and mountains, decided to separate entirely from either the United States or Canada and become a little nation of its own. In June, 1832, the Indian Stream Republic was formally begun, led by a man named Luther Parker. Four years later this so-called independent republic gave up and rejoined New Hampshire. In 1840 it was incorporated as the town of Pittsburg.

While all these events were taking place, another young lawyer named Franklin Pierce was rising to fame in New Hampshire and in the nation. Pierce was a native of Hillsborough and was born in 1804. When he was twenty-eight, he became a congressman. Before he was thirty-two he was elected to the United States Senate, the youngest senator ever to come from New Hampshire. A graduate of Bowdoin College in Maine, Pierce was a close friend of such other noted Americans as Henry W. Longfellow, Nathaniel Hawthorne, Calvin E. Stowe, and William P. Fessenden. During the Mexican War he served with the U.S. forces and became a brigadier general. In 1852 Pierce was nominated by the Democratic party for the presidency of the United States and was easily elected in November. The fourteenth President, Pierce was the only native of New Hampshire ever to serve in the White House.

Pierce was considered handsome and became widely popular for his personal magnetism as well as his abilities as a lawyer and legislator. He made no speeches in his presidential campaign—only a pledge of loyalty to his party. The death of his remaining son, 11 years old, in a railroad accident shortly after his election "completely unnerved" him and his wife so that he entered upon the heavy duties of the Presidency of the United States under a burden of nervous exhaustion.

During his administration, steps were taken for land purchases which would extend the power and consolidate the territory of the United States in future years: the Gadsden purchase of land for a railroad right of way to the Pacific; an attempt to purchase Cuba from Spain; efforts for the acquisition of Hawaii and a naval base in Santo Domingo; and inquiries were made of Russia about the purchase of Alaska. All of these enterprises did not reach fruition in Pierce's term of office, needless to say. His term as President was a difficult one, and he was glad to return to New Hampshire again in 1857.

COUNTRY LIFE BEFORE THE CIVIL WAR

New England farmers have long been known for their self-sufficiency and willingness to work hard. These two character-istics had ample scope for development in the period before the Civil War. The farmer could produce almost all his family's needs from his own acres and livestock: food, fuel, clothing, shoes, and tools. In the early years of the nineteenth century it was estimated that a farmer could "get by" if he earned as much cash as ten dollars a year; while as late as 1860 many farmers had no more than $100 a year in cash earnings. The men and boys worked from sunrise to sunset, and the winter months were just as busy as the summertime. The women

. . . picked their own wool, carded their own rolls, spun their own yarn, drove their own looms, made their own cloth, cut, made and mended their own garments,—made their own soap, bottomed their own chairs, braided their own baskets, wove their own carpets, quilts, and coverlids, picked their own geese, milked their own cows, fed their own calves, and went visiting on their own feet . . . and this last they frequently accomplished barefoot, carrying their only pair of shoes in their hands to save wear until they approached the meeting house.

Among the jobs that had to be done on most farms in New Hampshire was clearing stones from the land. One way of disposing of these stones was to build fence walls with them. Literally hundreds of miles of stone walls were thus con-structed by our forefathers. These stone walls were hard to build in the first place, and even harder to keep in shape after the winter's frosts had heaved them. Of this problem the famous New England poet, Robert Frost, wrote:

52

Something there is that doesn't love a wall,
That sends the frozen ground-swell under it.[4]

Men who built these stone walls for their neighbors in Danville, New Hampshire, in 1840 received between twenty-five and seventy-five cents a rod, depending on the difficulty of the work. (A rod is a little more than sixteen feet.) The purpose of a good stone wall was to be "pig-tight, bull-strong, and horse-high." In our time these walls are an abiding reminder of the days when ox teams and the hand scythe were a farmer's chief equipment.

Possibly because the effort to clear the land and prepare the fields for growing grain was so difficult, early in the nineteenth century a new type of agriculture became popular in New Hampshire. This was the raising of Merino sheep. These sheep, characterized by fine wool, were brought to the United States from Spain in 1808. The man who introduced them was an American named William Jarvis, who settled in Wethersfield, Vermont. His kinsman, Leonard Jarvis, brought the first Merino sheep into New Hampshire at Claremont in 1812. During the next thirty years enthusiasm for sheep-raising and the demand for wool steadily increased. In the middle 1830s more than one town in New Hampshire counted in excess of 10,000 sheep within its borders, while in the state as a whole by 1840 there were more than 600,000 sheep. This was the peak year, however, and after that the interest in sheep-raising declined.

Another interesting crop for the country people of New Hampshire during these years was the winter ice harvest. A noted businessman from Boston named Frederic Tudor began the practice of storing and shipping ice on a large scale. Tudor, when twenty-one years old, decided to send a cargo of ice to Martinique and, despite ridicule, sent a vessel to Saint-

4 From "Mending Wall" from COMPLETE POEMS OF ROBERT FROST. Copyright 1930, 1939 by Holt, Rinehart and Winston, Inc. Reprinted by permission of Holt, Rinehart and Winston, Inc.

Pierre in March, 1806. Although a long struggle for success in this unusual enterprise ensued, Tudor persisted, aided by Nathaniel J. Wyeth who had mastered the technique of ice cutting. Tudor finally developed a market for ice in warm and distant climates, sending it as far as Calcutta in 1833. By 1856 he was shipping 146,000 tons of ice from Boston, including some to China and Australia. Every New England village with an ice pond benefited. Hundreds of New Hampshire boys and men in the wintertime would cut ice from the rivers and lakes and transport this to Tudor's storehouses on the seacoast. A by-product of the ice business was the development of carbonated drinks, cooled by New England ice, which became known as "ice-cream sodas." By the time of the Civil War, the "soda fountain" had been introduced.

Fortunately for the New Hampshire farmer, there were forces at work which were to make his daily life easier and more profitable. Among these was the invention of farmers' magazines. One of the best was called the *Farmer's Monthly Visitor*. It was edited by Isaac Hill of Concord, New Hampshire, and the first issue was dated January 15, 1839. The *Old Farmer's Almanac,* begun in 1792 in Massachusetts, also furnished useful information to the farmer; while Dudley Leavitt of Meredith published a similar almanac with the same end in view.

Another factor that helped to raise the levels of farm life in the nineteenth century was the beginning of county and state "fairs." The first such fair held in New England occurred in Pittsfield, Massachusetts, in 1810. Four years later the Rockingham County Agricultural Society was chartered by the New Hampshire Legislature; it was followed by similar county-fair organizations in Cheshire County in 1816; in Strafford, Hillsborough, and Grafton counties in 1818; and in Coos County in 1819. Meantime, the New Hampshire state government began to make annual grants of money to these county-fair associations to encourage their work. In 1820 the legislature authorized the formation of a State Board of Agriculture, but this body really did little until 1870. From time to time, however, state fairs were held; one held in Manchester in October, 1851, was addressed by the great Daniel Webster, who had a handsome country place of his own in Franklin. These fairs helped farmers to learn about new breeds of livestock, such as the Morgan horse, introduced into New Hampshire in 1810, and the Guernsey cow, first brought to the state in 1831 from the British Isles.

A religious group known as the Shakers, of whom more will be said in the next chapter, was most helpful in developing new farm methods and introducing better standards of rural life into New Hampshire. Working from their headquarters in Enfield and in Canterbury, the Shakers showed the value of progressive methods in farming. They brought into the lives of the people whom they influenced many improved ways of doing things. They believed that a good diet contained milk, eggs, fruit, fresh vegetables, and they used the whole grain in making flour. They cultivated broom corn for the manufacture of Shaker brooms. They studied the herb plants of the forest and collected many of them which were useful to human beings. They made fine farm tools and other implements. As Mrs. Marguerite Melcher has said[4]:

In country-sides where the Shakers once dwelt, one finds in the older houses today Shaker clothes baskets, Shaker sewing baskets, Shaker boxes and sieves; and in the barns, Shaker grain measures, Shaker buckets, Shaker hay forks and rakes. It is a long time since any of these were made, but they are still strong, still being used.

Go West, Young Man!

In 1825 the Erie Canal in New York State was finished, and travel from the Hudson River to the Great Lakes became cheaper and more comfortable than ever before. Hundreds of New Hampshire folk, tired of the endless round of hard work

4 *See Bibliography referring to Chapter 5.*

on their stony hillsides, made up their minds to try for a new home in the rich and fertile lands of the midwestern states. One popular folk song expressed it this way:

> *Come, all ye Yankee farmers who wish to change your lot,*
> *Who've spunk enough to travel beyond your native spot,*
> *And leave behind the village where Pa and Ma do stay,*
> *Come, follow me, and settle in Michigandia——*
> *Yes, yea, yea,—in Michigan-d-i-ay!*

Another ran like this:

> *Way down upon the Wabash, such land was never known;*
> *If Adam had passed over it, the soil he'd surely own.*
> *He'd think it was the garden he played in when a boy,*
> *And straight pronounce it Eden in the state of El-a-noy.*
> *Then move your family westward,*
> *Good health you will enjoy,*
> *And rise to wealth and honor*
> *In the state of El-a-noy!*

To Michigan went New Hampshire people by the hundreds. John D. Pierce of Chesterfield, soon after his arrival in the new state, was elected superintendent of public instruction for Michigan. Cass County in that state was named after the famous Lewis Cass of Exeter, who had been Michigan territorial governor. It attracted many settlers from Exeter and Hopkinton. Zechariah Chandler, born in Bedford, became a loyal son of Michigan, and later was U.S. senator from that state.

And so it was with other states in the Great Lakes area. "Long John" Wentworth of Sandwich went to Chicago to become one of the leading citizens of that growing city. Joseph Glidden of Charlestown settled in DeKalb, Illinois, and there invented barbed wire, one of the great devices used for fencing the farms and ranches of the West. Beloit, Wisconsin, was started by a company of people from Colebrook who left in 1836 under the leadership of Dr. Horace White. James M. Goodhue of Hebron went to Minnesota in 1849; a county in Minnesota is named for him. Charles Hoag of Sandwich in 1852 moved to Minnesota and gave a little settlement there its present name, Minneapolis. John Sargent Pillsbury of Sutton went to Minneapolis in 1855 and began the flour mills that are now known all over the world. Hutchinson, Minnesota, was founded by three members of the Hutchinson family from Milford.

New Hampshire people went by covered wagon to the Pacific Coast or by ship around Cape Horn to the same destination. Hall J. Kelley of Northwood, a popular writer, made Oregon seem attractive to many New Hampshire residents. Daniel C. Corbin of Newport became a successful business leader in that state's chief city, Portland. The California city of Folsom was named for a New Hampshire pioneer, Joseph C. Folsom. The Reverend Samuel H. Willey of Campton was an early minister in San Francisco; and the Reverend Thomas Starr King, whose early life had been partly spent in New Hampshire—one of the White Mountains is named for him—also has a mountain named in his honor in California. Many New Hampshire people went to Salt Lake City with the Mormon immigrants after 1846.

Other New Hampshire people were lured to California by the report of the gold discoveries there in 1848. These gold seekers often traveled in "companies," and at least three well-known companies of this kind were formed in New Hampshire. On March 1, 1849, a departure for California took place from Boston. On board the ship "Sweden" that day were twenty-seven New Hampshire men. They had come from Salisbury, Walpole, Andover, Keene, Canterbury, and other places in the state. One of them, Moses Pearson Cogswell of Canterbury, kept a careful diary of his journey. We know that on this voyage the "Sweden" went all around South America and did not reach San Francisco until August 3, five months and two days after leaving Boston. So great was the outpouring of men hoping to make a fortune in the western gold fields that the census of 1860 showed more than 2500 people in California alone who listed New Hampshire as their native state.

Soon after the close of the War for Independence, the people of New Hampshire began to seek better ways of travel. In colonial times the traveler could ride by boat, canoe, or horseback, or he could walk, but there were few roads adequate for wheel travel. In 1796 the legislature authorized the beginning of the first "turnpike" in the state, to run from Durham to Concord, a distance of a little more than thirty-five miles. It was to be a toll road. A two-wheeled chaise pulled by one horse was charged one and a half cents per mile, while a four-wheeled wagon pulled by two horses was charged three cents per mile. This so-called "First New Hampshire Turnpike" was completed in 1797 at an average cost of $900 a mile. In 1799 the second New Hampshire turnpike was chartered to be built from Claremont to Amherst; the third New Hampshire turnpike began construction the same year from Walpole to Keene; while the fourth New Hampshire turnpike was begun in 1800 from Boscawen to Lebanon.

Interest in this type of road rapidly increased. Forty-seven turnpike companies were chartered between 1800 and 1810, and more followed in later years. The last such toll road was authorized by the legislature in 1893; it was the eighty-second turnpike in the state. By the middle of the century, however, most of these turnpikes had become "free roads," open to travel without charge and maintained by public authority. The only such turnpike in the state still operating as a toll road in 1964 was that up Mount Washington, chartered in 1853 and opened for traffic in 1861. The turnpikes were a great improvement over anything known in earlier years, and soon stage lines were running along their relatively smooth surfaces. The most famous of all the stagecoach factories was the Abbot Downing plant in Concord, which built hundreds of coaches, used all over the world.

At the same time that turnpikes and stagecoaches were changing and improving land travel, canal builders were making possible new kinds of travel by water. The Middlesex Canal, connecting Boston with the Merrimack River near Lowell, Massachusetts, was begun in 1793 and opened in 1803. Boats which came up the canal from Boston could then use the Merrimack River to points father north. The greatest trouble occurred at the several falls or rapids in the river. These had to be bypassed by more canals. For instance, a canal was built around Amoskeag Falls at modern Manchester and put into operation in 1807. Additional canals were then constructed at Hooksett and Bow, so that by 1815 the Merrimack River was usable all the way to Concord. Until the coming of the railroad this river-canal system was the chief means by which heavy freight was carried between New Hampshire and Massachusetts. A canal boat took at least seven days to make the trip from Concord to Boston, but it was much better than walking or riding horseback.

In the same way the Connecticut River was made navigable by canals. The rapids and falls near Bellows Falls and White River Junction were bypassed and by 1810 there was heavy traffic on that river. All kinds of freight went downstream, notably lumber and forest products; while on the upbound journey came the manufactured goods that the people in the inland regions so much needed. It was even proposed in 1816 that the Merrimack River be joined with the Connecticut River by a canal using the Contoocook River, Warner River, Lake Sunapee, and the Sugar River. But nothing was ever actually done about this suggestion.

As canals and improved rivers made travel by water easier inland, so new kinds of sailing ships made ocean journeys speedier and more comfortable. Portsmouth was the home port for many famous "clipper ships," some of the finest and fastest sailing vessels ever built. In one year, 1851, three renowned clippers were launched in shipyards at Portsmouth. One of these was the "Typhoon," which in 1851 sailed from New York to San Francisco around South America in 106 days. The second of these beautiful clippers, "Witch of the Wave," in

1853 sailed from Canton, China, to London in ninety days, a record seldom equaled. The third, the "Nightingale," in 1855 sailed from Shanghai to London in ninety-one days. Each of these three ships registered more than 1000 tons in weight and carried both freight and passengers.

CHANGES IN DAILY LIFE

One of the pleasant changes in the ordinary life of New Hampshire people in the first half of the nineteenth century was improved heating for the houses. All kinds of stoves and ranges were devised, the better to cook with and to keep the home comfortable. A Claremont inventor in 1816 made a new kind of cook stove, and others devised better heaters for the living rooms of a house. As stoves were improved, so were flatirons for ironing. Matches were first put into use in the 1830s, and whale oil and kerosene lamps came a little later.

The larger towns in the state were organized as cities. Manchester became the first city in New Hampshire by permission of the legislature in 1846. Portsmouth followed suit in 1849; Concord and Nashua in 1853; and Dover in 1855. With the growth of the cities came police departments, paved streets, street lighting, running water, fire departments, public parks, better schools, sewer systems, and much more that goes with city life. Manchester usually led the way in these ideas, but the other cities followed rapidly, and the old rural life steadily was modified by these "modern" developments.

In 1826 the so-called Lyceum was first organized in Massachusetts. This was a kind of adult education program which brought speakers, music, plays, and public discussions to all parts of New England. New Hampshire audiences heard such notable speakers as Wendell Phillips, Horace Mann, Henry Ward Beecher, and Charles Sumner. They listened to musicians like Jenny Lind, Adelina Patti, and Ole Bull. They were stimulated to start dramatic clubs, debating societies, libraries, and musical groups. In every city and larger town before the Civil War such organizations were active.

In 1852 Harvard and Yale held their first boat race near Center Harbor on Lake Winnipesaukee. Traveling showmen like Richard Potter—for whom Potter Place today is named— delighted New Hampshire audiences with their "magic." In the 1830s the first circuses began to travel through the state. Minstrel shows became popular in the 1850s, and a play like *Uncle Tom's Cabin* was acted out on scores of stages. "Spelling bees" pleased young and old alike, and even balloon ascensions were enjoyed in the summer months. One of the best liked of New Hampshire balloonists was a young man from Randolph named T. S. C. Lowe, who was to become nationally famous for his balloon work during the Civil War years.

In the seventy years which marked the period between President Washington and President Lincoln, our people witnessed all manner of changes in the pattern of daily living. Life became more varied, interesting, and many-sided.

6. *Manufacturing, Transportation, and Communications*

In colonial times industry and manufacturing were primarily small-scale activities, carried on largely in the home or in little mills located wherever water power was available. Present-day "factories," that is, large manufacturing enterprises situated in cities and towns, were not known in our state prior to 1800. The first steam engines, burning coal, were invented in England in the eighteenth century; in the history of their development the two most famous names were Thomas Newcomen and James Watt. The application of these engines to the operation of machinery and the concentration of power machines in large buildings brought about the factory system, or the Industrial Revolution. Historically speaking, this type of production first appeared in the textile industry of England, and a few years later in the United States.

In 1791, in Pawtucket, Rhode Island, a factory to manufacture cotton cloth began operating. It was designed by an immigrant Englishman named Samuel Slater, who later developed other textile factories elsewhere in New England, including some in New Hampshire. The first such mills were built in our state at New Ipswich shortly after 1800. In 1805 a man named Benjamin Pritchard started a small textile mill on the west bank of the Merrimack River in Goffstown. Five years later, Pritchard and others enlarged the mill and formed a company under the name of the Amoskeag Cotton and Woollen Manufacturing Company. Within twenty years it had become the biggest factory in New Hampshire, and one of the largest in the world. Until 1839 all its buildings were on the west bank of the river, but in that year a fine new plant was set up on the east side and called Stark Mill No. 1. Its mills on both sides of the river by 1850 employed more than 15,000 persons. They used upwards of 50,000,000 pounds of cotton a year and an almost equally large amount of wool. In full production they turned out cloth at the rate of a mile every minute of the working day. In the words of William Parker Straw[5]:

The Company was the heart and soul of Manchester—all values were dependent upon it—real estate of every description, merchandise of every sort and kind, for merchants and business men throughout the city depended upon the purchasing power of those who worked in the mills "under the hill." . . . Its trademarks were known throughout the United States, many of its brands were household words, so favorably known that no merchant considered his stock complete without a wide assortment of Amoskeag goods on his shelves.

This tremendous growth in the production of cloth and related products was not limited to the huge mills in Manchester. By 1850 there were fifty-six cotton manufacturing companies

5 *See Bibliography referring to Chapter 6.*

in New Hampshire, and sixty-one woolen mills. Cities and towns like Nashua, Dover, Exeter, Claremont, Newport, Lebanon, Keene, and Somersworth saw the growth of factories similar to but smaller than the Amoskeag mills. In Troy, Thomas Goodall after 1853 manufactured the best-known horse blankets in the United States. In places like Laconia and Franklin some of the first hosiery factories in the nation were functioning by the time of the Civil War. As Richard W. Sulloway has said[6]:

New Hampshire's part in the development of the latchneedle knitting machine was of outstanding importance and significance. The inventions of the Aikens, of Pepper, of Abel and of Scott and Williams entitle New Hampshire to a high rank in the roll of those states which have given to mankind technological achievements of far-reaching importance. I venture to say that these will remain as shining examples of that mechanical genius for which New England has been so famous.

That genius was soon applied to the production of other things such as shoes, leather goods, and wood and metal products. Rochester, Farmington, Derry, and other places developed large-scale shoe and leather factories. A mill in Sunapee made clothespins. Franconia had ironworks. A factory in New London, organized in 1835, produced scythes, axes, and hay knives. Fine paper was made in Alstead and West Claremont. Antrim developed a factory to make high-grade cutlery. In 1852 a group of men in northern New Hampshire started a mill in Berlin to produce wood products on a large scale; this later became the Brown Manufacturing Company. Penacook had a large flour mill; Andover a factory for making harnesses. Stratham produced engines, pipe fittings, and boilers. Manchester built steam locomotives and steam-powered fire engines that were known throughout the nation. Railroad-car factories were started in Laconia and Manchester.

Judged by present standards, in the new factories wages were

[6] See Bibliography referring to Chapter 6.

low and hours were long. About 1850 a common working day during the summer months was from sunrise to sunset, with time out for breakfast, luncheon, and supper—perhaps one and one half hours in all. This meant a working day of more than twelve hours. Wages for men might go as high as five dollars a week; women earned less; and children—for child labor was then permissible in New Hampshire—received as little as one dollar a week. In the 1850s the National Association of Cotton Manufacturers reported that the average annual wage of the New England worker was a little more than $200, which was greater than the average for similar workers in other parts of the nation. The Amoskeag Manufacturing Company erected large dormitory-like buildings in Manchester for its workers, especially for its women employees. Board and room charges were deducted by the company from the weekly pay of the worker. These charges averaged perhaps $1.25 or $1.50 a week. There were no labor unions in New Hampshire at this time and the state laws regulating matters like safety and working conditions were inadequate and poorly enforced.

Among the by-products of the new methods of manufacturing in New Hampshire were inventions of all kinds. One of the most famous of these was the sewing machine devised by Elias Howe in Nashua. Howe patented this machine in 1846; his patent number at the U.S. Patent Office was 4750—and this in the fifty-sixth year of that governmental bureau. Isaac Adams of Rochester patented new types of printing machines. The Aiken family in Franklin invented many ingenious machines for the making of hosiery. Members of the science faculty at Dartmouth College suggested methods of exploring for and testing the ingredients in petroleum, and thus in part led to the discovery of oil at Titusville, Pennsylvania, in 1859. T. S. C. Lowe assisted in developing better balloons and later pioneered in artificial refrigeration. Moses Gerrish Farmer of Boscawen made significant inventions in the field of electricity.

Thanks to the use of power machinery, large-scale extraction of various natural resources began in the state in the middle of the nineteenth century. A comprehensive survey of New Hampshire's mineral and other resources was made by state geologist Charles T. Jackson between 1841 and 1845. Among the resources which he studied was granite, especially at such places as Concord, Milford, Conway, and Lebanon. Power machinery made the cutting of this hard rock much easier than it had been in early years. Likewise, soapstone quarries were opened in Francestown; feldspar and mica mines were developed in Grafton, Sullivan, and Cheshire counties. Native ores, as we have seen, were smelted into iron at Franconia. Rock suitable for making grindstones and other sharpening machines was exploited in Pike, and abrasive garnets were found in Wilmot.

THE STEAMBOAT AND THE "IRON HORSE"

The steam engine, of course, could be used for many purposes other than the powering of factory machinery. One obvious use for it would be the propulsion of boats. Both in Europe and in the United States many inventors put their imaginations to work on this project. One of these was a man named Samuel Morey of Orford. Although the original steamboat in the United States was developed by Samuel Fitch on the Delaware River in 1786, Morey certainly was the second American to make this invention. In 1793 he successfully operated a small steamer on the Connecticut River both above and below Orford. This was many years before Robert Fulton carried out his experiments on the Hudson River in New York. Steamboats first appeared on the Merrimack River in 1814 and for a few years operated above and below Nashua. Steamboat navigation on the Connecticut River was flourishing in 1818; in 1831 one daring captain took his little steamboat as far up as the mouth of the Ammonoosuc River. The first steamer on Lake Winnipesaukee was built in 1833. By 1849 a handsome steamboat named "Lady of the Lake" began regular trips around New Hampshire's largest body of water. Later on, steamers were built to operate on other New Hampshire lakes, especially Lake Sunapee.

Even more extensive, however, was the effort to apply steam power to carriages to be used on the land. This meant the railroad. First invented and used in England, the steam engine on wheels, or the "Iron Horse," as it was soon called, appeared in the United States in 1829. By 1835 three short railroads had been built to operate out of Boston— the Boston & Worcester, the Boston & Providence, and the Boston & Lowell. Lowell was connected with Nashua in our state in 1838. Four years later the rails had reached Concord, and after that year railroad building in New Hampshire moved rapidly. In 1840 the state had fifteen miles of railroad track; by 1850 it had grown to 471 miles; and ten years later, in 1860, there were 661 miles.

This railroad mileage before the Civil War comprised almost as much trackage as there is left in New Hampshire in 1963 and included many lines that have now been abandoned. Rail connections between New Hampshire and Portland, Maine, were finished in 1842. The Northern Railroad from Concord to White River Junction was completed in 1848. The trackage across New Hampshire east and west through Berlin, Gorham, and Whitefield was opened in 1853. Littleton was connected with Whitefield in that same year. Shortly thereafter Manchester became the railroad "hub" of New Hampshire. By 1860 from Manchester one could travel by rail north to Montreal, south to Boston, east to Portsmouth, and west to Henniker. It was possible to reach Montreal by rail by two different routes: one through Franklin, Potter Place, Lebanon, and thence across Vermont; the other by Tilton, Laconia, Plymouth, and Woodsville. Going south, one could travel on one rail line through Nashua and Lowell to Boston; or by another line which took one to Boston by way of Lawrence and Andover, Massachusetts.

These fast-multiplying tracks of New Hampshire were built with the so-called "standard gauge," brought over from England; i.e., the rails were four feet, eight and a half inches apart. Until well after the Civil War the locomotives burned wood, and running times were relatively slow. Sunday railroad service was unlawful until the 1880s. Railroad ties were locally produced from the native forests. Rails were brought in either from British iron mills or sometimes from such American factories as the Mt. Savage Rolling Mills in Maryland. Telegraphy was not used in train operations in New Hampshire until the 1870s. "Through tickets" were first introduced between Boston and Montreal in 1851. A few years later a similar "through ticket" between Boston and Conway made possible combined railroad-steamboat-stagecoach travel between those two points. Mrs. Abraham Lincoln came this way when she visited New Hampshire in 1863. Many less famous tourists followed the same route.

In 1854, by treaty between the United States and Great Britain, special arrangements were made to carry mail and freight from the mother country to Canada. Steamships brought the freight and mail to Boston, and at that place they were loaded on special cars for shipment to Montreal by rail. In the days when no rail traffic was permitted on Sunday in New Hampshire, these special mail trains were the only exception to the rule. They were often objects of intense interest to the people who lived in the towns along the railroads. For instance, a Concord writer remarks that sometimes on a Sunday morning when the whistle of a mail train was heard, some people would quietly leave their church services to see the train go by!

The immense impression made by the coming of the railroad is suggested by some words uttered by Daniel Webster when he spoke in Lebanon on November 17, 1847:

It is an extraordinary era in which we live. It is altogether new. The world has seen nothing like it before. I will not pretend, nobody can pretend, to discern the end. But everybody knows that the age is remarkable for scientific research . . . The ancients saw nothing like it. The moderns have seen nothing like it till the present generation.

And about the same time Henry D. Thoreau in his home in near-by Massachusetts wrote:

I hear the iron horse make the hills echo with his snort like thunder, shaking the earth with his feet, and breathing fire and smoke from his nostrils.

New Developments in Communications

The telegraph, as all Americans know, was first put into use in the United States by Samuel F. B. Morse in 1844. Prior to that, Morse had made his living as an artist, and for some time had lived in Concord, New Hampshire. But his greater fame came from the application of electricity to the new science of telegraphy. Shortly after the idea had been proved practical, telegraph lines were built in our state. In 1847 the telegraph opened between Boston and Portland, Maine, crossing New Hampshire on the way. By 1850 Concord was linked by wire with the outside world. Ezra Cornell, who later contributed to what is now Cornell University in New York State, and who had worked with Morse, founded the Western Union Telegraph Company. Other telegraph companies were formed to compete with the Western Union.

It was not long before bold inventors projected the idea of laying a telegraph wire, properly insulated, on the bottom of the ocean, to connect the United States with Europe. First tried in 1858, this idea of a transatlantic "cable" did not permanently succeed until 1866. Suggestive of the popular interest in the cable, however, is a little verse written by a poet who was staying at Appledore Island in the Isles of Shoals in 1858. Benjamin Brown French wrote:

> Then bless the wire where now it lies,
> The ocean bed along, sir!
> Earth's greatest hope, the sea's great prize——
> Bless it in prayer and song, sir!

* * * * * *

Now in old Father Neptune's care,
As well as we are able
We place with shouts of joy and prayer,
The Atlantic Ocean Cable!

At almost the same time that the railroads and the telegraph lines were coming into New Hampshire, great changes were taking place in the handling of the United States mail. In the early years of the nation postal rates were high. After the law of 1816 a letter written on one sheet of paper cost six cents if its destination was not more than thirty miles away. If the letter had to go more than this distance, the rates would rise, reaching twenty-five cents if it had to travel as much as 400 miles. In 1840 the British first devised and used adhesive postage stamps. Seven years later Congress began the use of similar stamps in this country. Slowly mail rates were reduced. In 1851 the charge was lowered to three cents for a letter which traveled no more than 300 miles. Finally, during the Civil War, mail charges were made uniform by classifications, so that for "first-class mail" the charge was the same no matter what the distance the letter was to travel. During the Civil War, also, letter carriers were authorized for the larger cities and towns. But there would not be any R.F.D. or parcel-post services until years later.

Another important medium of communication was newspapers. New Hampshire, as we have seen, had its earliest newspaper in colonial times. In 1809 Isaac Hill began publishing the *New Hampshire Patriot* in Concord, a paper which under various names has continued to the present. In Keene the *New Hampshire Sentinel* had been started even earlier, in 1799. The Newport *Argus and Spectator* was established in 1823, while the Claremont *National Eagle* began in 1834. Other papers, a few still being published, many of them now gone, appeared in other cities and towns throughout the state before the Civil War and developed large and enthusiastic groups of readers. Most of these early newspapers were strongly in favor of one political party or the other, and all were "set" by hand. Published weekly, they rarely had more than four or eight pages.

Some New Hampshire-born newspapermen became nationally famous. Horace Greeley, a native of Amherst, in 1841 began the *New York Tribune,* soon to become one of the most influential newspapers in the country. Charles A. Dana, born in Hinsdale, opened his New York career working with Greeley, but later acquired the *New York Sun.* Stilson Hutchins of Whitefield founded the *St. Louis Times* in 1866, and a year or so later the *Washington Post* in our national capital. Charles G. Greene of Boscawen aided in starting the *Boston Post,* while George W. Kendall, like Greeley a native of Amherst, founded the *New Orleans Picayune.* Horace White of Colebrook became for a time the editor of the *Chicago Tribune.*

With the growth of railroads, telegraph lines, and newspapers, there came to be a real opportunity for the speedy transportation of parcels and perishable freight. Benjamin Pierce Cheney of Hillsborough in 1842 started an express company bearing his name to handle such service between Boston and Montreal. Steadily he expanded his business until in 1879 it became the American Express Company, operating from coast to coast in the United States. It was Cheney who presented to the state the bronze statue of Daniel Webster which still stands on the State House Plaza in Concord.

One of the most unusual men that New Hampshire has ever produced was Moses Gerrish Farmer, born in Boscawen. Excited by the development of the railroad and telegraph and by other inventions, Farmer turned his mind to the possibilities of employing electricity in many ways. In 1847, using a crude system of storage batteries, he ran a little backyard electric railroad behind his home in Dover. In 1851 he was retained by Boston to install in that city a system of automatic fire alarms. This he put into operation that same year, making it possible for any citizen to signal a fire simply by pulling the lever on an alarm box. Actuated by electricity, the fire-alarm box would register the location of the fire on a central panel in the fire station. In 1856 Farmer discovered how to send more than one telegraph message over a wire at the same time—multiplex telegraphy. In 1868 he lighted a house in Cambridge, Massachusetts, by electricity, thus anticipating Thomas Edison by eleven years. Later on, he applied his knowledge of electricity to naval devices for the United States.

7. *Plain Living and High Thinking*

New Hampshire saw many earnest efforts for popular reforms in the years between the winning of independence and the beginning of the Civil War. Most such reforms were of nation-wide concern, and what took place in this state reflected and paralleled what happened in the rest of our country during the same period.

One of these movements was to secure greater rights for women. In colonial days, women lacked many of the basic privileges which now we take for granted. For example, women did not vote; they did not go to college; they did not take an active part in business; and they did not have the same property rights as men. This appeared to many to be very unfair, and various strong-minded women began efforts to remove these limitations. One such woman was Sarah Josepha Hale. Born in Newport, New Hampshire, in 1788, she became editor in 1837 of the most famous woman's magazine of her day, *Godey's Lady's Book.* Mrs. Hale unceasingly used her pen to urge greater rights for women and to make women more energetic participants in public affairs. She heartily endorsed the historic "Declaration of Women's Rights," set forth at a meeting in Seneca Falls, New York. She urged more practical types of women's dress. She constantly supported the latest ideas in public health and medical care, including the use of anesthesia after its discovery in 1846. She gave space in her magazine to women writers.

Mrs. Hale herself wrote one of the first American novels, entitled *Northwood,* in 1827. Even better known was one of her poems written for children:

> *Mary had a little lamb; its fleece was white as snow;*
> *And everywhere that Mary went, the lamb was sure to go.*

She encouraged the writing of the famous New Hampshire poet, Celia Laighton Thaxter, who spent so many years on the Isles of Shoals.

Another reform of interest to New Hampshire people was the matter of temperance in the use of liquor. The New Hampshire Temperance Society was organized in 1828. Dartmouth College had a noted branch of this group, founded and led for many years by Dr. Dixi Crosby of the medical school at that institution. One popular song for young folks in this state ran as follows:

> *Oh, then resign your ruby wine,*
> *Each smiling son and daughter.*
> *There's nothing so good for the youthful blood,*
> *Or sweet, as sparkling water.*

In 1855 New Hampshire passed a strict liquor control law modeled after that then in force in Maine.

74

Following the War of 1812, many New Hampshire people became interested in the possibility of world peace. Dr. Noah Worcester, then a minister in Salisbury, published a notable essay on the folly of war. Peace societies were soon started in towns like Exeter, Hollis, Salisbury, Boscawen, and Portsmouth. After Dr. Worcester came two other peace leaders, Samuel Elliot Coues of Portsmouth and William Ladd of Exeter. In 1840 Ladd published a remarkable book entitled *An Essay on a Congress of Nations for the Adjustment of International Disputes Without Recourse to Arms.* Many modern students see in the United Nations of our day the realization of the hopes of Ladd and his contemporaries.

Better care for the unfortunate members of society was another concern in New Hampshire. In 1813 a new state prison was built in Concord, and as early as 1834 one of our governors, William Badger, recommended that the death penalty be abolished and the most severe penalty be limited to life imprisonment. The great work of Dorothea Dix in urging hospitals for the treatment of the mentally ill was reflected in the opening of the New Hampshire State Hospital in Concord in 1842. The idea of better care for juvenile offenders was suggested by the founding of the State Industrial School in Manchester in 1856. Private efforts to provide help for the blind, the deaf, and the aged were started, but public action was not taken until much later. One of the most remarkable persons ever born in New Hampshire, however, Laura Bridgman of Hanover, became the first famous patient at the Perkins Institute for the Blind, established in 1831 in Boston.

The New Hampshire Medical Society is one of the oldest in the nation. Founded in 1791, it helped to start the Dartmouth Medical School in 1798. For many years this well-known institution did much to stir interest in better health, personal and public, in New Hampshire. One of its original faculty members was Dr. Nathan Smith, who later assisted in starting the Yale Medical School and the Medical College of the University of

Vermont at Burlington. New Hampshire doctors were quick to accept anesthesia after its first successful use in Boston in 1846.

THE GROWTH OF EDUCATION AND OF PUBLIC LIBRARIES

Until well after the Civil War the public elementary school of eight grades was the basic tax-supported educational institution of New Hampshire. The first public high school in the state was started in Portsmouth in 1830. But this kind of school did not develop much until the state legislature passed a special law in 1848. The State Department of Education was started in 1846. The first person to be named to the new position of Commissioner of Common Schools was Professor Charles B. Haddock of Dartmouth College. A few years after he assumed his new post, there were 2294 separate school districts in the state. The average monthly cash salary for male teachers was $16.42; for female teachers it was $7.18. The number of children enrolled in the "district schools" of the state was 87,825, and the total amount of tax money spent on them was $212,324. Of these country and small-town schools it has been said:

The typical one-room school of the middle nineteenth century had no sanitary facilities, no electric lights, no furnaces. Pupils seated near the heat—whether a fireplace or its "modern" successor, the round wood-burning stove—used books and handkerchiefs to protect their faces from the intense blaze, while those at the other end of the room still shivered in spite of heavy winter clothing. Books and other school supplies were scanty. All grades, with pupils of all ages and sizes, were grouped together in one room. It was not unusual for the teacher to be smaller—and younger—than some of the students.[7]

On April 3, 1854, the New Hampshire State Teachers Association was founded in Manchester by two teachers from that city. The original constitution provided only for male members, but women were admitted in 1876. The first annual meeting of

[7] *See Bibliography referring to Chapter 7.*

the group, held in Nashua in November, 1854, stated its purposes to be ". . . personal acquaintance, mutual improvement, and professional cooperation in the work of disseminating knowledge and improving the mind."

Aside from the small number of high schools in the cities, the usual secondary school in New Hampshire was the so-called academy. By 1850 there were more than ninety such privately controlled academies in the state. More than 7000 boys and girls were enrolled in these academies that year. The oldest and most famous was Exeter Academy, started in 1783. Some of the others have long since closed, but a few remain to this day. Among these are Kimball Union Academy at Plainfield, founded in 1813; Pinkerton Academy at Derry, begun in 1814; Colby Academy at New London, chartered in 1837; Proctor Academy in Andover, started in 1848; and St. Paul's School in Concord, opened in 1856. These academies were the basic college preparatory schools for New Hampshire youth, and from them boys might go to various institutions. After 1837, a few girls went on to Mt. Holyoke, the first women's college of New England.

Dartmouth College in Hanover, of course, was the only institution of its kind in New Hampshire until after the Civil War. It drew young men from all parts of the nation. In 1842 the graduating class numbered ninety-two, the largest to that year ever to graduate from the college. Dr. Nathan Lord, president from 1828 to 1864, gathered an able faculty around him and made the institution notable. During that period the inclusive expenses of a Dartmouth student for four years—tuition, board, room and clothes—might total $700.

In the field of public libraries, New Hampshire was a leader in the entire country. In 1818 a room was set aside in the new State Capitol Building at Concord which was to become the start of the present New Hampshire State Library. Meantime, "social libraries" were started in many towns. These were incorporated by act of the state legislature and were really private libraries, established by groups of interested persons in the several towns. The first such "social library" was organized in

Dover in 1782, and within thirty years more than 150 had been incorporated in New Hampshire. In 1822 Dublin established the first tax-supported juvenile library, open to all the children of the community. Eleven years later Peterborough carried this idea to its logical conclusion: in 1832 it opened the first true public library in the United States, tax-supported, for the free use of all citizens of the town. In 1849 the state legislature passed a law encouraging this kind of public library and authorizing any town to do what Peterborough had started.

CHURCH AND STATE

When the New Hampshire constitution of 1784 was written and adopted by the people of the state, it was assumed that the support of the church should come from taxes. People paid taxes to support the church just as they paid taxes for any other town endeavor. It was not strictly speaking, however, a "state church" that was implied. Each town by a majority vote at the annual town meeting could decide what denomination was to be the tax-supported one for that community. In New Hampshire this usually meant the Congregational Church. But this was not always the case. In some towns the Baptist Church was the tax-supported one; in others it might be the Presbyterian Church; and in one or two towns it was the Episcopal or even the Quaker.

Many New Hampshire people, however, especially after the adoption of the First Amendment to the U.S. Constitution in 1791, began to feel that the towns through their tax money should not support any church. Rather, they felt, the support of the churches should come only from voluntary gifts of the members. In 1819 in the Toleration Act of that year, the state legislature tried to place New Hampshire churches on a voluntary basis. While not canceling any ministerial contracts then in existence, this law made more difficult any future use of tax money for church support and gradually led to the typical "separation of church and state" which most Americans today believe to be correct. In the passage of this law, many prominent men like former Governor William Plumer and newspaper editor Isaac Hill played an active part.

Of the fourteen commonly recognized Protestant denominations in 1800, New Hampshire had churches of exactly half: Congregational, Baptist, Presbyterian, Methodist, Episcopal, Universalist, and Quaker. In later years, however, many other religious groups entered the state. Among these were the Unitarians, Millerites, Shakers, Mormons, and Roman Catholics. Unitarians were usually an offshoot of the Congregational faith and became active in New Hampshire after 1830. The Millerites were prominent in the 1840s; they believed that the end of the world was coming on October 22, 1844. The Shakers founded a colony at Canterbury in 1792 and the one at Enfield in 1793. The Mormon faith was popular in New Hampshire in the 1830s and 1840s, and a number of people from our state accompanied Brigham Young on the long journey to Salt Lake City in 1846–1847.

The Shakers may be mentioned in a little more detail because the last members of their group still live in Canterbury today. They were followers of a remarkable Englishwoman named Ann Lee. Organizing in Canterbury and Enfield, they numbered at one time many hundreds of people. As they did not believe in marriage, there were no children to carry on the faith after the older generation died. They felt that the twelve basic virtues of life were: faith, hope, honesty, continence, innocence, simplicity, meekness, humility, prudence, patience, thankfulness, and charity. They lived in the two villages of Enfield and Canterbury, and at one time their farm buildings were among the largest in the state.

As late as 1835, Roman Catholics in New Hampshire numbered about 700 persons. Ten years later there were twice that many. By 1884 their number had reached 45,000, and Pope Leo XIII established the Diocese of New Hampshire with its headquarters in Manchester. The immigrants who came to the state from Ireland after 1846 and from Canada a few years later were invariably members of the Roman Catholic faith. With them they brought parochial schools and hospitals.

In the 1840s German immigrants introduced the custom of the Christmas tree, and a few years later English immigrants began for the first time to observe Christmas by sending out Christmas cards.

Two other remarkably interesting religious practices appeared in New Hampshire in the early 1800s, both transplanted from England. One of these was the Sunday school. The first such training program was started in Rhode Island about 1795, but fifteen years later Sunday schools were functioning in many New Hampshire towns. In 1852 the first Y.M.C.A. ever known in New Hampshire was founded in Portsmouth. A few months later that same year another Y.M.C.A. was started in Concord. These two were among the first ten Y.M.C.A. groups started in all North America. Shortly after the Civil War the sister organization, the Y.W.C.A., first appeared in our state.

Many churches in New Hampshire in the early part of the nineteenth century acquired church bells from the Revere Foundry in Boston, established by Paul Revere. Although Paul Revere died in 1818, his firm continued to make church bells until 1827. There are still sixteen congregations in our state which are proud to have "Revere bells" in their church towers. Keene and Newport have two each; Effingham, Hampton, Hampstead, Hancock, Hopkinton, Manchester, Milford, Newfields, New Boston, New London, North Hampton, and Walpole have one each.

A Congregational church service in Bennington, New Hampshire, in the 1840s was described in the centennial history of that church in 1939. It might be typical of church services in many parts of the state for the period:

. . . the House was heated by two stoves in the vestibule with a funnel from each passing through the house to the chimneys beside the pulpit, giving little heat to any part of the body except the head. Many brought hand-stoves, soapstones and sandbags to keep their feet from freezing. There were two services each Sabbath one hour and a half long with an intermission of one hour for Sunday-School and lunch. The congregation was expected to stand during prayer that occupied half an hour or more . . . The singers being in the gallery, we stood, turned around and looked at them twice during the services. The music accompanying them was a bass viol and two fiddles. There was no means of lighting the house except oil lamps and tallow candles brought in from adjacent houses.

The nineteenth century saw great expansion of the foreign missionary movement of the Christian church. Devoted men and women from our state and from other parts of the United States sought to go to the newly-opened countries of Asia or Africa to teach the people there the basic truths of the Christian religion. Among the noted missionaries from New Hampshire were John Taylor Jones of New Ipswich who went to Siam, where he worked with the same people made famous in the moving picture called *Anna and the King of Siam;* Sarah Hall Boardman Judson, who went to Burma as the devoted wife of the eminent Adoniram Judson; and Levi Spaulding of Jaffrey, who gave much of his life to the people of Ceylon.

THE FINE ARTS

As mentioned earlier, Samuel F. B. Morse painted some of his best-known works in New Hampshire about 1820. Thirty years later another New Hampshire artist named Benjamin Champney founded at North Conway what came to be known as the "White Mountain School." This was a movement to stress the importance of showing nature in its beauty and love-liness. Dozens of young men accepted Champney's ideas, and many of their paintings survive today. Both the New Hampshire State Library and the New Hampshire Historical Society have originals by men who learned their art in the "White Mountain School." Two other painters, Adney Tenney and U. D. Tenney, made many portraits of New Hampshire's noted men of the past and of their own day. More than fifty portraits by these two artists now hang in the State Capitol in Concord.

The best-known musical group in New Hampshire prior to the Civil War was the "Singing Hutchinsons" of Milford. This family choir of more than a dozen brothers, sisters, and cousins, made repeated tours throughout the United States and abroad. One of their favorite songs, "Kind Words Can Never Die," was as familiar throughout our nation in the 1850s as any popular song today. Another musician closely associated with the Hutchinsons was Walter Kittredge of Merrimack, whose "Tenting Tonight on the Old Camp Ground" became one of the never-to-be forgotten songs of the Civil War.

In addition to Sarah Josepha Hale and Celia Thaxter, two distinguished New Hampshire writers mentioned earlier, another famous writer at this time was Thomas Bailey Aldrich of Portsmouth. His *Story of a Bad Boy* was read and enjoyed by thousands then and is in print today. James T. Fields, also of Portsmouth, contributed to "the flowering of New England" by becoming one of the most remarkable publishers the world has ever seen, according to one authority. He was a partner of the Boston firm of Ticknor and Fields, a writer, a literary patron, an editor of the *Atlantic Monthly,* and a friend of well-known authors on two continents. He wrote a poem called "The Owl Critic" which has delighted people ever since.

"Artemus Ward" (Charles Farrar Browne), the American humorist, served on the staff of the *Coos County Democrat* at Lancaster for many years. Longfellow, Hawthorne, and Whittier came often to New Hampshire, and many of their stories and poems are laid in this state. Perhaps most famous are Hawthorne's story entitled "The Great Stone Face" and Whittier's poem, "New Hampshire, 1845."

During these lively and busy years before the Civil War, organized summer tourist travel to New Hampshire began. Abel Crawford built the first trail up Mount Washington in 1819. Nine years later he built the first hotel in the Crawford Notch part of the state. In 1840 Horace Fabyan opened a bridle path up Mount Washington, along the same general route followed by the later cog railroad. The first "Summit House" was erected atop the big mountain in 1852. Meantime, tourists were beginning to come into southern New Hampshire around Mount Monadnock and into the central portions near Lake Winnipesaukee and Lake Sunapee. Henry David Thoreau three times came to Mount Monadnock between 1843 and 1860, and from the hotel at the top of this mountain Ralph Waldo Emerson wrote:

> *Every morn I lift my head,*
> *See New England underspread*
> *South from St. Lawrence to the Sound,*
> *From Katskill east to the sea-bound.*

8. *New Hampshire and the Civil War*

Although New Hampshire had permitted slavery during the colonial period, by the early 1800s state sentiment was clearly opposed to it. In 1820, for example, the New Hampshire Legislature passed a resolution which fairly expressed the feeling of most people at that time:

Slavery is prohibited by the immutable law of nature, which is obligatory as well on states as individuals. The establishing or permitting slavery by a State, being thus morally wrong, the right to do it, instead of being essential to its sovereignty, cannot exist, except only in cases where slavery having been already introduced cannot be suddenly abolished, without great danger to the community. Under such circumstances, it must of necessity be tolerated for a time as the sole means of self preservation. This painful necessity may justify the temporary continuance of slavery in certain States of the Union, where it now exists. But . . . nothing can justify the unnecessary extension of this great evil to newly formed States.

During the forty years which ensued, this feeling persisted in New Hampshire. Anti-slavery societies were founded in many cities and towns; church groups passed resolutions disapproving it; and men like Nathaniel P. Rogers of Portsmouth and Stephen S. Foster of Canterbury took the lead in building up anti-slavery sentiment. The agitation over the admission of Texas as a slave state in 1845 excited much response in New Hampshire, well expressed by an influential congressman from Dover named John P. Hale. In a bitter election campaign in 1846 Hale was elected U.S. senator from New Hampshire. From his Senate seat he continued his opposition to the extension of slavery into new states or territories of the United States. The passage by Congress of the so-called Compromise of 1850, which seemed to many in New Hampshire to favor slavery, caused an emotional outbreak. Even the great Daniel Webster, who had voted for this compromise legislation, was savagely criticized.

On October 12, 1853, fourteen New Hampshire leaders, with varying political backgrounds, met in Exeter. There they organized a new anti-slavery political party to which they gave the name, Republican. Thus began the famous party which along with the Democratic party has lasted as one of the two major political groups in the United States. Among the Exeter leaders were Senator John P. Hale; Amos Tuck of Exeter—a friend of Abraham Lincoln; George G. Fogg of Concord, a newspaper editor; and William Plumer of Epping, a son of a former governor. This new Republican party elected its first governor in 1857 and for years thereafter was the dominant political group in the state.

In the early months of 1860 Abraham Lincoln came to New Hampshire to make some speeches on the invitation of his old friend, Amos Tuck. In addition to his wish to please Tuck, Lincoln desired to visit his eldest son, Robert, who in the autumn of 1859 had entered Exeter Academy. Lincoln reached Exeter on Wednesday afternoon, February 29, 1860, and spent the night there with his son. On Thursday, March 1, Lincoln went to Concord where he spoke to a large meeting in the afternoon; that same evening he addressed an even larger group in Manchester. At this meeting, Lincoln was introduced by the mayor of Manchester as "the next President of the United States." On Friday night, March 2, Lincoln spoke in Dover, and on Saturday evening he made his fourth and last speech at Exeter. On Sunday, March 4, he attended church in Exeter with Robert and the next day started home. One year from that Sunday he was to take the oath as President of the United States.

In the presidential election of November, 1860, a decisive majority of New Hampshire voters cast their ballots for the Republican candidate, Abraham Lincoln. In the months between his election and his taking the oath of office—in those years Presidents were inaugurated on the fourth of March following their election—New Hampshire people watched with amazement and shock the secession of many southern states from the United States. There followed the formation of a new nation called the Confederate States of America, and threats of war between North and South.

After Lincoln took the oath of office as President, five uneasy weeks followed. On April 12, however, the crisis finally came. Southern troops fired on the United States garrison in Fort Sumter, Charleston, South Carolina. Three days later, President Lincoln called for 75,000 volunteers to put down the rebellion. New Hampshire's share was to be one regiment of 780, enlisting for ninety days. The men who hastened to volunteer for the army did so primarily because they felt that their beloved nation was in danger of being destroyed. Secondarily, some of them believed that the moral evil of slavery must be eliminated from the country.

When the Civil War began, New Hampshire's militia was not very well trained. In theory this comprised all able-bodied men between eighteen and forty-five years of age. In fact, it was limited to twelve military companies scattered throughout the state. These companies boasted picturesque names like the Amoskeag Veterans (Manchester); the Newcastle Light Guards; the Canaan Grenadiers; the Westmoreland Rangers; the McCutchins Guards (New London); the Wilson Artillery (Keene); the Mechanics Phalanx (Pittsfield); and the Granite State Guards (Great Falls). The total number of men in these twelve companies may have been about 800.

Following the appeal for a regiment of volunteers from New Hampshire, recruiting offices were opened at twenty-eight places in the state, and within two weeks 2000 enthusiastic men had volunteered. This was many more than necessary for one regiment, so that very shortly additional regiments were authorized. The original ninety-day service period was soon changed to a three-year term. Between 1861 and 1865, New Hampshire furnished eighteen regiments of infantry. In addition several hundred men volunteered for cavalry duty, for special units like Berdan's Sharpshooters, for artillery companies, and for naval service. The total number of individuals from this state who served the Union exceeded 33,000. Since our New Hampshire population by the census of 1860 was only 326,073, it is apparent that more than ten per cent put on a uniform. Casualties—killed, wounded, missing, and discharged for disability—totaled thirty per cent. The eighteen regiments were numbered in numerical order. Book-length histories of each of them have been written, except for the Tenth New Hampshire. One should read some of these to understand the courage and achievements of our troops in the Civil War.

Perhaps the best known of the eighteen regiments from New Hampshire was the Fifth. Commanded by Colonel Edward E. Cross of Lancaster, it played a heroic part in the Battle of

Gettysburg in July, 1863, where Colonel Cross was killed. Well known among other officers who had been born in New Hampshire were Major General Benjamin F. Butler, a native of Deerfield; Major General John A. Dix, a native of Boscawen; Brigadier General Fitz-John Porter, a native of Portsmouth; and Brigadier General Benjamin F. Kelley, a native of New Hampton. Distinguished naval officers from our state included Rear Admiral George E. Belknap of Newport; Rear Admiral Enoch G. Parrott of Portsmouth; Rear Admiral George H. Wadleigh of Dover; and Commodore George Hamilton Perkins of Hopkinton. A handsome statue of the last-named officer now stands on the west side of the State Capitol building in Concord.

The brilliant young T. S. C. Lowe of Randolph, New Hampshire, whose earlier work with balloons has been mentioned, became the founder of the original U.S. Air Corps. In June, 1861, Lowe persuaded President Lincoln that the use of balloons for reconnaissance purposes would greatly help the U.S. armies. Lincoln authorized Lowe to undertake the organization of a balloon corps, and the young scientist promptly did so. By the end of the year he had constructed five military balloons for the United States. Each of these balloons was filled with hydrogen gas and was held firmly to the earth by a strong towline. When an ascent was made, the observer was in the balloon basket. The rope was unwound, and he went up perhaps 2500 feet. Then by telescope he studied the earth beneath and in front of him. Whatever he saw in the way of enemy operations he would report to the ground by means of a telegraph instrument attached to his equipment in the basket. In this fashion in many battles in the early years of the war, valuable information was passed from the sky to the earth. In the summer of 1863, Lowe became ill and had to retire from the army. His balloon corps did not continue after that time.

In the spring of 1861 the Portsmouth Navy Yard launched two new ships for the U.S. Navy. One was named "Kearsarge"; the other was called "Ossipee." The U.S.S. "Kearsarge" eventually became one of the most noted ships in the Navy. For three years later it was successful in sinking the notorious Confederate cruiser, the "Alabama," which for two years had been at sea destroying more than fifty merchant ships which flew the American flag. Commander of the U.S.S. "Kearsarge" was Captain John A. Winslow. After the war Captain Winslow built a hotel on the slope of Mount Kearsarge in the town of Wilmot and made it a popular place for summer visitors. The hotel was twice burned, once in 1867 and again in 1899. After this second destruction it was not rebuilt, but its site is now part of the Mount Kearsarge State Park.

PROBLEMS ON THE HOME FRONT

The people of New Hampshire made many contributions to the war effort of their men in uniform. In June, 1861, the New Hampshire Soldiers' Aid Society was organized, with Mrs. Mary S. Perley of Concord as its president. This group supplied boxes of socks, clothing, bandages, mittens, canned and dried fruits, and much more in the way of gifts for the troops. The society was affiliated with the national organization called the U.S. Sanitary Commission. It did for the fighting men the same kind of work that the Red Cross was to do in later wars. A similar organization called the U.S. Christian Commission—like the USO of modern times—was likewise heartily supported by New Hampshire people. This organization maintained reading rooms for the soldiers in army camps, distributed religious materials, and established "coffee wagons" and "diet kitchens" where hot drinks and snacks could be served.

The U.S. Sanitary Commission assisted in bringing nurses to the sick and wounded soldiers on the battlefields and in the hospitals. In the spring of 1861 President Lincoln designated the famous Dorothea Dix to serve as Superintendent of Female Nurses. Congress provided that these women of mercy should receive for their services three meals and forty cents a day while on duty. From many thousands of women who sought appointment as nurses, Miss Dix and her staff selected about 3200 in all. The best-known New Hampshire nurse so chosen was Miss Harriet Dame of Concord. She went into the service in 1861 and remained a valued member of it for four years. Miss Dame believed strongly that sick men needed the comforts of home and liked to get wounded soldiers sent back to New Hampshire for recovery. As she put it in a letter: "I frequently find a New Hampshire soldier with some disease that requires the tender treatment and pure air of home in order for his recovery."

Many New Hampshire doctors made their way into the military ranks. At the beginning of the war the entire medical staff of the U.S. Army consisted of 115 medical men. By 1865 there were more than 10,000 physicians and surgeons in uniform. Among the best known of these doctors from New Hampshire were Dr. John M. Brown of Hinsdale; Dr. Luther V. Bell of Francestown; Dr. Dixi Crosby of Hanover; and Dr. George F. French of Dover. The government established a huge military hospital at Manchester, which was called the Webster Hospital. It was not continued after the war, and today its site is a part of the northern section of that city. In 1864 the United States approved the so-called Geneva Convention, by which fighting nations agreed not to molest the hospitals and medical work of the enemy.

An interesting problem arose as the presidential election of 1864 approached. This was the question of whether men far from home in the army or navy could vote; in other words, it was the problem of "absentee voters." By 1864 seventeen of the northern states had passed legislation permitting this kind of voting by men in uniform. In August, 1864, therefore, at a special legislative session the New Hampshire Legislature did likewise. In the presidential election that fall Abraham Lincoln received more than three times as many votes from the "boys in blue" as did his nearest opponent.

Another matter affecting the home front was how best to assist the wives and children of the men who were far away on the battlefields. In 1862 the legislature passed a law requiring each town to render financial assistance in such cases. The payments were to be four dollars per month to the wife, and two dollars for each child, but in no case should the total amount of aid exceed eight dollars in any one month. In 1864 in some parts of the state, sugar was thirty-five cents a pound; butter was fifty cents a pound; kerosene was $1.50 a gallon; beans were five dollars a bushel. Obviously there must have been a great deal of voluntary help to the soldiers' families to make it possible for them to keep going.

Taxes were high during the war, and a national income tax was introduced in this country to help finance the costs of the conflict. In 1863 the U.S. government established "national banks," and the first such organizations were started in our state. In 1863, also—thanks largely to Mrs. Sarah Josepha Hale's efforts to persuade the President to do so—the government began the practice of a national Thanksgiving Day on the fourth Thursday of November each year. In 1862, at the instigation of a New Hampshire-born man, Henry Wilson of Farmington, then a U.S. senator from Massachusetts, Congress established the Congressional Medal of Honor. During the great conflict more than fifty New Hampshire soldiers or sailors won this award for valor over and beyond the call of duty. The Amoskeag Company in Manchester produced war materiel, including rifles for the army and textiles for clothing and uniforms. Other factories in the state did likewise.

New Hampshire Government during the War

The four men who served as governors of New Hampshire between 1861 and 1865 were all members of the Republican party. The first, Ichabod Goodwin of Portsmouth, was governor in 1861 when the war began. He backed Lincoln's call to arms and assisted in raising the first regiments of volunteers. In June, 1861, Nathaniel Berry of Hebron became governor and was re-elected in 1862. He was friendly with President Lincoln and cordially cooperated with the national government. In

1863 Joseph A. Gilmore of Concord was named governor, being re-elected in 1864. Governor Gilmore was keenly interested in the welfare of the fighting men and sought in every way to make their lot more comfortable. In 1865 Frederick Smyth of Manchester was elected governor, serving in this office when the war ended and welcoming the men back home.

During Governor Gilmore's administration Mrs. Abraham Lincoln, the wife of the President, visited New Hampshire. She came to the state in August, 1863, with her two sons, Robert and "Tad," and spent a week in the White Mountain area near Conway. Twice she took the Mount Washington carriage road to the summit and was most enthusiastic about the magnificent scenery from that peak. She later wrote that after the war was over she wanted to bring her husband with her to see the same sights. But, as we know, this was not to be. Governor Gilmore welcomed Mrs. Lincoln to the state, but she did not take part in any public programs or events while here.

In 1864, Abraham Lincoln ran for a second term. The friends of the President in New Hampshire were determined that he should carry the state again as he had done in 1860. A rising young political leader from Warner named William E. Chandler took the lead in this movement. His efforts were successful, and Lincoln won a decisive majority in our state in November, 1864. Just prior to the election, Salmon P. Chase, Secretary of the Treasury for three years under Lincoln, but out of the presidential Cabinet as of June, 1864, visited New Hampshire. Chase had been born in Cornish, was a graduate of Dartmouth, but at this time was a resident of Ohio. He made a long trip through the state in the early autumn of that year, and his detailed diary of what he saw is still interesting reading.

Former President Franklin Pierce lived throughout the war years in Concord. He was, of course, a Democrat and therefore normally opposed to the Republican party and its leadership. But a deep sense of patriotism inspired him to support much of the war effort. He made only three speeches during the years between 1861 and 1865: once immediately after the Fort Sumter incident; a second in July, 1863; and the third a tribute to President Lincoln after the death of the latter in April, 1865. Pierce was a man of great courtesy and kindness; his real character was well expressed in a letter he wrote President and Mrs. Lincoln after the death of their second oldest boy, Willie, in the White House in February of 1862. This beautiful letter was for the first time published in 1947.

Because of his many ties of friendship with New Hampshire people, President Lincoln named a number of men from our state to high public office during the war. For example, John P. Hale in 1864 was appointed U.S. Minister to Spain. George G. Fogg was designated Minister to Switzerland. Nehemiah G. Ordway of Warner in 1861 became sergeant at arms of the U.S. House of Representatives and held this position for twelve years. William E. Chandler in the spring of 1865 was named to a high post in the U.S. Navy Department. The most noted member of the New Hampshire delegation to Congress during the war years was Edward H. Rollins of Concord. Other men from our state who held high positions under President Lincoln included his old friend, Amos Tuck of Exeter.

After the end of the war in April, 1865, the government of New Hampshire began a long effort to show appreciation to the men who had served their state and their country through the years of the conflict. Governor Smyth took the lead in paying this deserved tribute. At his request in 1866 the legislature authorized all cities and towns to establish monuments to honor both the war dead and the returning veterans. In 1868 the state adopted May 30 as Memorial Day to be observed each year. In 1875 the legislature established the Hall of Flags in the rotunda of the State Capitol, where the flags of the Civil War regiments from New Hampshire have ever since been on display. Finally, in 1895 the legislature authorized the publication of a massive work by Adjutant General Augustus D. Ayling, *Revised Record of the Soldiers and Sailors of New Hampshire in the War of the Rebellion*. This is the official listing of every man from our state who served the nation during the Civil War.

In tribute to New Hampshire's part in the American Civil War, Edna Dean Proctor, a poet from Henniker, wrote in 1873:

Land of the cliff, the stream, the pine,
Blessing and honor and peace be thine!

And still may the hill, the vale, the glen,
Give thee the might of heroic men,
And the grace of women pure and fair
As the May-flower's bloom when the woods are bare.

Land of fame and of high endeavor,
Strength and glory be thine forever!

9. *Politics and World Wars: 1865–1945*

In the fifty years between the close of the Civil War in 1865 and the first World War, twenty-six different men occupied the governor's chair in Concord. Twenty-four of these were Republicans. The two Democrats were James A. Weston of Manchester (1871–1872, 1874–1875) and Samuel D. Felker of Rochester (1913–1915). The State remained basically solid in its adherence to the party that had been founded here in 1853 but occasionally in times of economic difficulty it swung its support to the principal opposition party. Each of the twenty-six governors served two years in office.

Until the late 1870s the term of a governor of New Hampshire was twelve months only. In the constitutional convention of 1877, however, the term was changed to two years. Ratified by the voters of the state, the new system was put into effect for the first time after the election of 1878, when Natt Head of Hooksett became governor. In the same amendment to the original constitution of 1784, the time of choosing the governor was changed from town-meeting time in March to the regular November election in even-numbered years. New Hampshire is unique in that by law it must have periodic conventions to consider constitutional amendments. In addition to the constitutional convention of 1877, other such assemblies were convened in 1889, 1902, and 1912. These resulted in further minor changes to the basic law of the state. New Hampshire continued to have the largest legislature in the nation, with most of its towns being represented in that body. Town meetings in March retained their old-time flavor and were vital institutions of democracy.

During this fifty-year period many "third parties" appeared on the American scene, but none of these ever drew substantial support in our state. In the 1870s the Greenback party, advocating a national issuance of paper money, and the Prohibition party, standing for a very strong anti-liquor law, each succeeded in winning a few thousand votes in New Hampshire. In 1884 the Equal Rights party, urging the granting of the right to vote to women, gained a few followers. In the 1890s the Populist party attracted some voters. Basically, however, New Hampshire remained what it had always been: a two-party state, with the Democrats usually in the minority. Of course, such a dominance by one party was not altogether healthy and there were frequent charges that the Republicans maintained their power by methods of "boss control." One of the well-known Republican leaders in the state was a man named Ruel Durkee from Croydon. He was vividly described in the famous novel *Coniston* by a writer named Winston Churchill. In this book Durkee appears under the name of Jethro Bass.

Many efforts were made between 1865 and 1915 to modernize the governmental organization of the state: In 1865 the legislature established the New Hampshire Fish and Game Commission, one of the first such governmental bodies in the nation. In 1871 the Board of Agriculture—renamed the Department of Agriculture in 1914—was authorized. Ten years later the privately sponsored Society for the Protection of New Hampshire Forests was founded to speed up the conservation of the woodlands of the state. In 1911 Congressman John W. Weeks, a native of Lancaster, but then living in Massachusetts, sponsored an important law. By this statute national forests were authorized in various parts of the eastern United States. Under this law the White Mountain National Forest was started in New Hampshire in January, 1914. It was gradually expanded until it covered more than ten per cent of the total land area of the state.

Until well after 1900 the chief political issue in New Hampshire was the alleged control which the great railroads exercised over government and the elected representatives of the people at Concord. In those days the railroads were the only form of speedy transportation. Consequently, most passenger and all freight traffic had to move on them, and the powerful companies which controlled this vital transportation system were in a position to exert much influence on government. For example, railroad companies could, and did, grant free passes to their favored friends in the legislature.

A fierce determination to oppose this powerful railroad influence in government led to the formation of the Lincoln Republican Club in New Hampshire in 1906. The very first item on their program was a demand for a law that would stop the issuance of railroad passes to any persons except company employees. Such was the official beginning of the Progressive Movement in New Hampshire. This reflected a nationwide expression of feeling against the power of big business in politics, and for the creation of new agencies of government to help the "common man." Winston Churchill, the author of *Coniston,* was the first candidate of the Lincoln Republican Club for governor. He failed to be nominated in 1906 and in 1908. But in 1910 a Progressive candidate from Peterborough named Robert P. Bass won the Republican nomination for governor and was elected that November. He successfully pushed through the legislature a number of important reforms. These included the establishment of the Public Utilities Commission, the State Tax Commission, a Workmen's Compensation Law, and other significant measures. Although he was not re-elected in 1912, the momentum of reform continued into the next administration of Democratic governor Samuel D. Felker.

After the Civil War, New Hampshire went Republican in every presidential election until 1912. In that year the Republican party split into two factions, and in so doing lost to the Democratic candidate, Woodrow Wilson. In New Hampshire the split in the Republican party proved as damaging as it did elsewhere in the nation, and for the first time since 1852 the electoral vote of our state went to the Democrats.

The best-known Republican leaders of New Hampshire on the national political stage were William E. Chandler of Warner and Jacob A. Gallinger of Concord. Chandler had been a friend of Lincoln and remained influential in the Republican party. He served as Secretary of the Navy in the Cabinet of President Chester A. Arthur from 1882–1885. He supervised the building of the first four steel cruisers of the U.S. Navy and aided in founding the Naval War College at Newport, Rhode Island. In 1889 he began the first of two six-year terms in the U.S. Senate. Two years later Jacob A. Gallinger was elected as the second senator from New Hampshire and served until 1917, the longest term in that office that any New Hampshire man ever has held. A hospital in Washington, D.C., today is named after him.

Secretary of State John Hay in the 1890s bought an estate on Lake Sunapee in Newbury, and until his death in 1905 spent many weeks there each summer. From the Hay summer retreat came the letters and instructions which set in motion some of the famous episodes in U.S. diplomatic history, such as the Open Door Policy in 1899 and 1900. President Theodore Roosevelt came to our state in 1902 to visit his Secretary of State. In 1905 President Roosevelt selected Portsmouth, New

Hampshire, as the meeting place for diplomats from Japan and Russia. These two countries had been fighting a costly war in distant Manchuria during 1904–1905, and both appealed to the President of the United States to help them make a peace settlement. At Portsmouth, New Hampshire, therefore, the official treaty ending the Russo-Japanese War was signed on September 5, 1905.

The Spanish American War in 1898 and the Philippine War from 1899 to 1902 marked the growth of U.S. influence in international affairs. (More than a thousand men from New Hampshire volunteered to serve in Cuba or in the Philippines.) This necessarily involved the rapid growth of the U.S. Navy. One of the newest and most powerful warships yet built was christened "New Hampshire" as it was launched at Camden, New Jersey, in 1906. In 1913 and again in 1915 New Hampshire was the location of the "summer White House." President Wilson rented the estate of Winston Churchill in Cornish and with his family spent as much time as possible in our state during the summers of those years. Mrs. Wilson* later wrote:

He was like a boy home from school, when he could steal a week-end away from Washington and come there to the peace and quiet of the hills. When we walked we would try to forget that lurking behind every tree was a Secret Service man. We would go, always a car full of us, on long motor rides through that lovely country, exploring new roads and sometimes very bad ones, getting back in the late twilight for tea on the terrace, or stopping at a picturesque little teahouse en route; then a late dinner, after which the best part of the day would come.

With the curtains drawn to shut out the cold night air, we would gather before a fire, and together read the latest dispatches sent from Washington, from Europe, from Mexico, from everywhere. The President would clarify each problem for me and outline the way he planned to meet it.

* From My Memoir, copyright 1939 by Edith Bolling Wilson. Reprinted by permission of the publishers. The Bobbs-Merrill Company, Inc.

The outbreak of what we now call the First World War on August 1, 1914, shocked the people of New Hampshire. As the Claremont *National Eagle* said in its leading editorial a week later: "We Americans stand aghast at the warlike demonstrations of Europe." President Wilson officially stated the attitude of our country on August 19 when he wrote: "The United States must be neutral in fact as well as in name." Former President Theodore Roosevelt, a man greatly admired in our state, declared on September 23: "We should remain entirely neutral and nothing but urgent need would warrant breaking neutrality and taking sides one way or the other." These sentiments were echoed by the majority of citizens in New Hampshire.

But almost from the beginning it became clear that neutrality was going to be difficult. On May 7, 1915, off the coast of Ireland a German submarine sank a British passenger liner, the "Lusitania"; 1,198 persons were drowned, including 114 Americans. Many of our people were horrified and angered by this and other actions of the German armed forces. Slowly there grew the feeling that our country might some day have to "go in." In May, 1916, a huge Preparedness Parade took place in New York City, and our state was represented by what was then said to be the "largest American flag in existence." It was 100 feet long, fifty-two feet wide, and had been made ". . . every stitch of it, by The Amoskeag Manufacturing Company." U.S. General Leonard Wood, a native of Winchester, was urging men to volunteer for summer military training camps, and many New Hampshire citizens did so. President Wilson, endorsing "preparedness," won his campaign for re-election in 1916. He carried New Hampshire, however, by just sixty-four votes. Early the next year the German government stated that even American ships would not be respected in its submarine warfare. President Wilson promptly asked Congress for a declaration of war on Germany. On April 6, 1917, Congress complied with his request. In its leading editorial the next morning the Manchester *Union* said: "NOW OUR TIME HAS COME." Once again the United States was involved in a major war.

The U.S. government planned to build its new army by a system of conscription, or the "draft" as it was called. On June 5, 1917, all men in the United States between the ages of twenty-one and thirty "registered" and received a serial number. There were 10,500 numbers in all, repeated in the 4500 registration places throughout the nation. On July 20, 1917, the Secretary of War drew the first number from a container holding the 10,500 numbers. It was 258. Thereupon every man in the United States with that number became liable for service. A year later, in 1918, Congress expanded the draft ages to cover the years from eighteen to forty-five. During the war 8900 draftees from our state were inducted into the army, and many more volunteered for the armed services. Most of the New Hampshire draftees served in the 26th, or Yankee Division. They trained at Camp Devens in Massachusetts. The Yankee Division reached France in late 1917 and took part in many of the great battles of 1918. Total New Hampshire armed services deaths in World War I numbered 697.

The home front during 1917–1918 saw many innovations. College campuses became military training camps, as the men students drilled in special classes. Daylight Saving Time was introduced into the state and nation in 1918 in an effort to save coal. "Meatless days" and "heatless days" were promoted to save food and fuel. Taxes sharply increased. War gardens were encouraged in every schoolyard. A state-wide organization was set up to sell war bonds, and New Hampshire people bought more than $75,000,000 worth of such securities. The American Red Cross had thirty chapters in New Hampshire, and the people of the state responded heartily to their appeal. Millions of bandages and dressings were prepared, and more than $1,000,000 in cash contributions were made. Other societies like the Salvation Army, the Y.M.C.A. and Y.W.C.A., the Knights of Columbus, the Federation of Women's Clubs, and the War Camp Community Fund carried out their programs in the state. Early in the war Governor Henry W. Keyes of Haverhill named a Committee on Public Safety under the chairmanship of John Jameson of Antrim, and this group of 100 coordinated the war effort of New Hampshire.

On November 7, 1918, came the exciting news that an armistice had been signed. This was quickly proved to be a false report, but actually the armistice was signed just four days later. On November 11, 1918, therefore, the great struggle was over.

Most New Hampshire servicemen were in their country again by the following summer, and July 4, 1919, was Homecoming Day in many a community in our state. The legislature of 1919 decided to build a huge bridge across the Piscataqua River between Portsmouth and Kittery, Maine, as a War Memorial and to place an impressive plaque in the Capitol, honoring the war dead of the state. The lawmakers also voted a $100 bonus to each New Hampshire citizen who had served in the war. Eventually 19,425 claims were paid.

The effort of President Wilson to bring into being a League of Nations to prevent future world wars occupied the attention of many Americans during the months after the cease-fire. When he brought the treaty—including the constitution of a League of Nations—from the peace conference in Paris, he presented it to the U. S. Senate for approval. One of the most persistent opponents of Wilson, the League of Nations, and the treaty was U. S. Senator George H. Moses of New Hampshire, who was opposed to any "entangling alliances." Because of this attitude of Senator Moses and his like-minded associates, it was impossible to get the required two-thirds vote of the Senate, and the United States did not join the League of Nations. In 1920 the Democratic presidential candidate, James M. Cox, running on a promise of support for and friendship to the League of Nations, was heavily defeated. New Hampshire followed the majority of her sister states in returning that year to the Republican party fold. In this election, thanks to the adoption that summer of the Nineteenth Amendment to the U.S. Constitution, women voted on a large scale for the first time in New Hampshire.

ECONOMIC STRAIN AND NATURAL DISASTERS

Wars are often followed by periods of economic distress. This proved to be so after the First World War, and the first effects were noted in New Hampshire in 1920. In December the Amoskeag Manufacturing Company of Manchester announced that for an indefinite time its operations would be at only half-time, and wages in the factory would be much reduced. Other mills in the state followed suit. Thirteen months later, early in February, 1922, the Amoskeag Company announced a further reduction in wages and a longer working day for the employees. Again other textile mills did likewise. Ten days later came the most extensive strikes in New Hampshire's history. Workers in Manchester and in other textile cities across the state insisted that they would not return to their jobs until better treatment was offered.

But nine months later the beaten strikers went back to work again. The terms on which they resumed were no better than had been offered in February, and the effect on the manufacturers was to be disastrous. Indeed the textile business in New Hampshire has never fully recovered from the prolonged and costly labor troubles of 1922. In 1930 came more strikes. Five years later, on December 24, 1935, the Amoskeag Corporation filed a petition in bankruptcy. Despite the shock to public opinion, the next year the mills, the equipment, and other property were sold off to the highest bidders. A group of leading New Hampshire businessmen, organized under the name of Amoskeag Industries, bought many of the old buildings and began a long and ultimately successful effort to lease or sell them to new and smaller companies. Within ten years more than a hundred new business firms were using the property, and among them hiring more working people than the former Amoskeag Manufacturing Company had ever done. This was the so-called "Miracle of Manchester," which in the long run turned apparent economic disaster into improvement.

In 1922 the Democratic candidate, Fred H. Brown of Somersworth, was elected governor on the strength of his pledge to support the forty-eight hour week and labor unions in general. He began programs for the improvement of labor conditions which were followed by his successor, Republican John G. Winant. Winant, when he took the oath of office in 1925, was the youngest governor in the United States, being just past thirty-five years old. He was noted for his compassion toward the poor and needy. Of his attitude as governor it was later written:

He made it a rule as governor to see all who wanted to see him; his door was open to everyone in the State. As a result, the corridors at the Capitol were always crowded with persons waiting to speak with him. His sympathies with his callers and their difficulties tempted him not to hold them to the 10 or 15 minutes his secretaries allotted. In consequence, he was almost invariably behind his schedule, sometimes hours behind. This despite the fact that he arrived at his office early, worked through the lunch period—sometimes he sent out for a sandwich and coffee; frequently he went without anything—and often remained late in the evening. He secured shorter hours for others, not for himself. After these long periods at the office, he always took home a brief case filled with papers to look over at night. Sometimes he would return to his office after dinner and work until well past midnight.[8]

New Hampshire people showed their appreciation by re-electing him in 1930 and again in 1932. He was the only three-term governor in the last century.

During the interim between Winant's first and second terms, in November, 1927, the state was ravaged by severe floods. The western towns and counties were badly injured by the rampaging waters, and the state legislature was forced to appropriate $3,000,000 in emergency relief and assistance. Nine

[8] *See Bibliography referring to Chapter 9.*

years later, in March, 1936, came more terrifying floods which covered even more of the state's area. This time the direct and indirect damages to New Hampshire were estimated at more than $25,000,000. From the disastrous experiences of these two great floods came the extensive system of dams and flood-control reservoirs which have been built by state and U.S. funds since 1938.

As if floods were not enough in the way of natural disaster, in September, 1938, the worst hurricane in recorded history swept across New England. Estimated damages in New Hampshire alone from this windstorm went as high as $50,000,000. Millions of board feet of timber were blown down, and salvage operations took years. Scores of miles of railroad trackage were washed away, and much of it has never been rebuilt. City parks lost hundreds of their finest trees. Many churches saw their steeples blown completely off the towers. Electrical lines and telephone lines were so severely smashed that it was weeks before service could be restored in full. Other hurricanes have come to the state since 1938, but this was the worst.

To this burden of industrial trouble and natural disaster was added the "great depression" which afflicted the United States after 1929. Beginning in October of that year, the depression carried the economic activity of the country steadily downwards until the middle of 1932. Between 1930 and 1940 in only one year, 1937, did the U.S. total of unemployed drop below 8,000,000. In New Hampshire in 1931, one out of every five workers was out of a job.

In 1933 the New Deal began under President Franklin D. Roosevelt. Although a Republican, Governor Winant cooperated heartily and a great many New Deal projects were undertaken in New Hampshire. The Civilian Conservation Corps (CCC) built camps in our state. The Works Progress Administration (WPA) undertook many constructive endeavors, including a history of New Hampshire, prepared by unemployed writers. The Federal Deposit Insurance Corporation (FDIC) became a part of most of the state's banks. Other programs were devised to help in finding employment for many in New Hampshire.

In 1934 Republican Styles Bridges won the governorship, going from that post to the United States Senate in 1936. Four times re-elected, Bridges remained in the Senate until his untimely death in 1961; during these years he achieved national recognition and importance. During his governorship, on the argument that it would provide extra income, the state legalized the race track at Rockingham Park.

Under the next governor, Francis P. Murphy, the New Hampshire State Police was created in 1937; the handsome State Office Building in Concord was built; and the first lines of the Rural Electrification Authority were brought to the state. In his second term, the beautiful mural paintings by artist Barry Faulkner were placed on the walls of the State Senate Chamber.

New Hampshire's Part in the Second World War

Despite their worries at home, New Hampshire people had watched with real anxiety the rise of the European dictators: Benito Mussolini in Italy after 1922; Joseph Stalin in Russia after 1925; and Adolph Hitler in Germany after 1933. The aggressive military efforts of the Japanese army and navy in Asia following 1931 were likewise observed with concern by our people. When the Second World War began on September 1, 1939, the Concord *Monitor* stated in its leading editorial:

We feel certain that try as hard as we may, we cannot stay out of the war if it is at all prolonged.

It was a prediction that would prove true.

By 1940 New Hampshire public opinion on the war was split into three main groups. There were those who felt that, come what may, our country should stay out of the great war abroad. This was the position of the America First Committee and its followers. There were those who felt that we should help the nations fighting against Hitler and Mussolini, but not formally go to war. This was the attitude of the Committee to Defend America by Aiding the Allies and its members. And, finally, there were those who thought we should get into the war as soon as possible. This was the feeling of the Fight for Freedom Committee and its supporters. All three of these groups were active in our state and, by radio, newspaper advertisement, and mass meetings, sought to persuade the people to their views.

In 1940 Franklin D. Roosevelt ran for the presidency for the third time and was easily re-elected. New Hampshire had not voted for him in 1932, but did so in 1936, and again in 1940 and in 1944. In the autumn of that year, a Selective Service law much like the draft of 1917–1918 went into effect. On the first registration day, October 16, 1940, all men in the state between the ages of twenty-one and thirty-six were tabulated. Before the end of the war in 1945, more than 36,000 men had been inducted by the draft, and more than 22,500 had entered the service by volunteering or from the organized reserves. A total of about 60,000 New Hampshire citizens wore their country's uniform between 1940 and 1945—about the same percentage of the state's population as in the Civil War. Total deaths among New Hampshire's servicemen and women between 1941–1945 were to number 1599.

The wartime governor of our state was Robert O. Blood of Concord. Early in 1941 he secured from the legislature the authority to organize a State Council of Defense. This consisted of twenty-five leading citizens, and under their direction more than 200 local defense councils were organized. In 1942 Noel T. Wellman of Kearsarge was named chairman of the Council of Defense. Under his direction the many committees and subcommittees smoothly coordinated the war effort of New Hampshire. When the stunning news of Pearl Harbor flashed across the nation and the state on Sunday afternoon, December 7, 1941, the people were ready for whatever action might be necessary.

As in the First World War many feats of valor were performed by New Hampshire men in the army, navy, air force, and marine corps. Three men from the state won the Congressional Medal of Honor: Captain Harl Pease of Plymouth (for whom Pease Air Force Base in Newington is now named); Sergeant C. H. Karaberis of Manchester; and Commander Richard H. O'Kane of Durham. Marine Private Rene A. Gagnon of Hooksett was one of the six men immortalized in the famous photograph of the raising of the American flag on Iwo Jima in the Bonin Islands in February, 1945. New Hampshire men "flew the hump" into China, stormed ashore on the Normandy beaches on June 6, 1944, crossed the Rhine in March, 1945, and participated in naval and air battles in every combat theater.

The economic effect of the war on New Hampshire was great. At long last, unemployment disappeared, and productivity in the factories and mills made new high records. As a New Hampshire historian Philip Guyol says[9]:

For five years people worked more, produced more, earned more, saved more, and spent more than ever before in their lives.

Many a New Hampshire firm was awarded the coveted "E" for excellence by the U.S. government. One of the best-kept secrets of the war was the development of the so-called "proximity fuse" by an electrical company in Dover. Agricultural productivity increased almost as much as industrial. Between 1939 and 1945 the cash value of food and farm products in our state more than doubled.

With greater earning power than ever before came new demands upon the people's generosity. The Red Cross, now organized in thirty-nine chapters, produced more than 16,000,000 surgical dressings and did notable "Home Service" work. The United Service Organizations Inc.—a merger of the Y.M.C.A., the Y.W.C.A., the Salvation Army, the Knights of Columbus, the National Jewish Welfare Board, and the National Trav-

[9] See Bibliography referring to Chapter 9.

elers Aid Association—maintained servicemen's clubs in the state at Manchester, Portsmouth, and Claremont. In 1944 the annual drive in New Hampshire for the support of the USO secured $464,000 on a quota of $414,000, giving our state first place in the nation in percentage of money raised. The eight "drives" for war bonds brought in more than $539,000,000 from New Hampshire people and business firms, or more than $1000 per person for every man, woman, and child in the state.

Other aspects of the war effort may be noted. The Office of Price Administration (OPA) handled the problem of rationing and distributed the ration coupons and books to the people as justice demanded. Hundreds of so-called Liberty ships were constructed in shipyards across the country. Among those named for notable New Hampshire men and women were the "Josiah Bartlett," "Daniel Webster," "John Sullivan," "Henry Wilson," "John A. Dix," "Robert Rogers," "Jacob Gallinger," "Susan Colby," and "James T. Fields." The Portsmouth Navy Yard built many types of ships for the fighting fleet, among these eighty-two submarines between 1940 and 1945 inclusive. The colleges of the state gave all manner of special courses to aid the war effort.

In 1944 a great international conference was held at Bretton Woods in the White Mountains to prepare plans for the International Bank for Reconstruction and Development and for the International Monetary Fund, both to be established after the close of the war. In March, 1945, New Hampshire people in their annual town meetings voted their opinion on the Dumbarton Oaks plans for a world organization to replace the old League of Nations. New Hampshire was the only state in the nation to undertake such an official poll of public opinion. The people voted approval of the new world organization (now the United Nations) by a majority of more than two to one. When the Charter for the United Nations as drawn up at San Francisco was submitted to the Senate for approval in July, 1945, both New Hampshire senators—Bridges and Tobey —voted in favor of it.

With the end of the war in Germany in May, 1945, and the end of the Japanese war in September of that same year, New Hampshire people looked forward to the return of their men and women in uniform. Governor Charles M. Dale, who had been elected in November, 1944, urged the legislature to take every step possible to make easy the veterans' return to civilian life, and this was done. Two state trade schools were organized to help the men in learning vocations. A bonus of $100 was voted for each veteran. A State Reemployment Commission tried to fit the men and women back into peacetime jobs with a minimum of difficulty. It was later estimated that ninety-eight per cent of all veterans in New Hampshire made a satisfactory adjustment to civilian life. By the end of 1945 the people of the state were looking forward to a time of peace and prosperity and were seeking to put behind the memories of the trying years through which they had just passed.

10. *Eighty Years of a Changing Economy*

Transportation

In 1865 there were 700 miles of main-line railroad trackage in New Hampshire; by 1920 this had grown to 1252 miles; but by 1945 it had dropped to barely 900 miles. During the eighty years between 1865 and 1945 the steam railroads saw both their greatest popularity and a rapid decline to their present limited use.

In the great days of the railroads, however, many remarkable engineering feats were accomplished. For example, in 1869 a steam train began operating to the top of Mount Washington. This inclined cogwheel railroad, still functioning, was the first of its kind in the eastern United States. It was the result of the inventive imagination of Sylvester Marsh of Littleton and Herrick Aiken of Franklin. In 1875 the mountain line through

Crawford Notch was finished, and trains began using this spectacular route. In 1912 Canadian bankers proposed a new railroad to be built from Montreal to Boston, running in part through New Hampshire; but because of the First World War this project was never carried out.

The Boston and Maine Railroad introduced Centralized Traffic Control (CTC) near Dover in 1930 and bought its first Diesel locomotive in 1934. The first lightweight streamlined train ever seen in New Hampshire, the so-called Flying Yankee, began operating in 1935. This was at the very time when the splendid locomotives of the Boston and Maine—called by the schoolchildren of the area "Cardigan," "Salem Witch," "Old North Bridge," "Camel's Hump," and "Allegash"—were still in use. Within fifteen years they would be gone forever. It was the railroads which brought the idea of "standard time" to New Hampshire in 1883.

New Hampshire had a few "horse-car" trolleys. But these were soon abandoned in favor of the electric trolley car. Dover led the way in electric trolley cars by starting a line in 1890. Soon Concord, Manchester, Nashua, Exeter, Portsmouth, and Claremont had trolley systems. In 1902 an "interurban electric" line began operations between Concord and Manchester. Later this system was extended so that a traveler could board an electric trolley in Penacook and, by using transfers, go from there to Nashua, or to Exeter, or to Portsmouth. By the time of the First World War this interurban trolley system was widely developed all over the eastern United States. It was possible in 1914, for instance, to go from Boston to New York by trolley car and, for most of the way, between New York and Chicago. As rapidly as they had been built, however, the trolley lines were abandoned. Manchester saw its last trolleys in 1940.

The coming of the motor car stopped the growth of steam and electric railroads and put the minds of New Hampshire people on a new and more private way of travel. In 1895 there were only four operable automobiles in the entire United

States and none in our state. The question of how it was to be powered—whether by gasoline, by steam, or by electricity—slowed the development of the automobile for a few years. Some people thought that steam would be the best source of power for an automobile, and the Stanley Steamer, built in Newton, Massachusetts, was very popular in New Hampshire for a time. In fact, a Stanley Steamer was the first automobile ever to drive up the carriage road on Mount Washington to the summit on August 31, 1899. But eventually the gasoline-powered car prevailed.

When in 1905 New Hampshire began issuing automobile number plates to car owners, 704 cars were registered that year. Ten years later the number had grown to more than 13,000, and the State Highway Department was established. The next year, 1916, the first federal Highway Act was passed, and the beginning of U.S. Highways took place. The state first imposed a gas tax of one cent a gallon in 1923. This rose steadily until by 1945 it was four cents a gallon. Since then it has increased to seven cents, and the federal tax is added to that. Filling stations, road maps, bus lines, motels, and other characteristics of the motor age became commonplace in New Hampshire life. And year by year better roads were built. The first concrete highway in the state was put down in Hooksett in 1918. Highway signs began to appear after the First World War. Traffic lights were introduced early in the 1920s, and superhighways were on the drawing boards by 1945.

The first airplane seen in New Hampshire was in 1911 when a small plane was flown from Waltham, Massachusetts, to Laconia; the next year a seaplane landed successfully on Lake Sunapee. The First World War stimulated a rapid expansion of air activity, and in 1925 an effort to carry the mail by air was made in the area about Laconia. The year of Lindbergh's famous flight across the Atlantic, 1927, the first city airport of the state was begun, the present Grenier Field in Manchester. Six years later Northeast Airlines started the first regular passenger service through the state. Beacon towers were installed in many parts of New Hampshire, and they began winking their lights to aid night-time flying.

As motor cars and airplanes increased in New Hampshire, the old-time steamboats on the lakes began to lose their appeal. On Lake Sunapee, for instance, in 1910 there were five excellent steamers, one of them, the "Armenia White," capable of carrying 600 passengers. Lake Winnipesaukee likewise had many steamers. But by the end of the Second World War there were only two or three left on Lake Winnipesaukee. An old steamboat man has written:

On a beautiful July morning in 1910, as the steamboat "Armenia White" was swinging into Sunapee Harbor, Captain Frank Woodsum blew the whistle signal from the pilot house. The writer was the Purser on the "White" at that time, and the whistle meant that Captain Frank wanted to see me in the pilot house.

As I entered the door, the Captain said: "Do you see what I see there at the dock?" I took the glasses and looked, and there at the landing stood the first Model-T Ford we had seen in Sunapee. Captain Frank, arms folded and steering the ship with feet and knees, as he so often did, said solemnly, "There, my boy, is the end of the steamboat." How right he was.

OTHER FORMS OF BUSINESS

During much of this period there was a continued growth of the historically basic industries of New Hampshire: textiles; shoes and leather goods; wood and forest products; and metalworking. Nashua at one time had the largest blanketmaking mill in the world. Laconia built great factories for the making of hosiery machinery. Plymouth, Lisbon, and Littleton made gloves. Jaffrey had a plant which came to produce forty per cent of all the tacks made in the nation. Boxes were made in Winchester. Paper mills grew up in Berlin and in Claremont. Rochester became a center of the fiberboard industry of the state. Fine furniture was produced in Milford and Keene.

Ready-to-wear garments were made in Lebanon, Newport, and Meredith. Leather goods were produced in Concord. One of the great inventors of American history, Albert Ball, established a factory at Claremont for producing rock-cutting machines and coal-mining devices. In the 1880s Benjamin W. Kilburn in Littleton made more stereoscopic slides than any other man in the United States. In addition to these business activities, New Hampshire developed a number of major insurance companies, particularly in the field of fire insurance. The cities of Manchester, Concord, Keene, and Portsmouth were insurance centers of our state.

The production of electricity for light and power was made possible by a series of inventions, many of them by Thomas A. Edison, in the late 1870s and 1880s. In 1882 Berlin was the first place in New Hampshire to experiment with electric lighting. Nine years later Manchester boasted that it was ". . . one of the best-lighted cities in the United States." In the beginning every city or town developed its own electric company, but soon these were merged or consolidated into large power corporations. The Public Service Company of New Hampshire by 1945 represented the combination of more than eighty one-time small companies. These large companies sought permission to build dams on our rivers and thus to create water power for generating electricity. Among the first such hydroelectric power dams were those on the Merrimack and its tributaries. By the 1920s new and even larger dams were being built along the Upper Connecticut River. The great Comerford Dam near Monroe was finished in 1930, and power lines were soon carrying high-voltage electricity from this dam all the way to Boston.

The telephone, invented in 1876 in Boston, was brought into our state a year later in Manchester. By 1882 the first telephone company in that city had 375 subscribers. In 1893 there were about 1500 telephones in the state. As telephone lines reached into the country areas, the old-time isolation of the rural districts lessened. As Harold F. Wilson says[10]:

10 *See Bibliography referring to Chapter 10.*

It even made possible a general conversation in which a representative from each family in the neighborhood could join, for the telephones were usually connected to one line which served a whole district. Moreover, there was no means of excluding any particular family from the discussion, for by taking down the receiver as soon as a ring was heard on the line, any person could hear what was going on, and the "click, click, click," as one receiver after another was removed, gave warning of the unannounced presence of numerous listeners. Long before the day of the radio, hill-country families had learned how to "tune in." The telephone benefited the farm family economically as well as socially. For example, the farmer no longer had to kill a dozen chickens, take them to town by team, and sell them for whatever the storekeeper was willing to give. He could now call his prospective customers and ascertain how many chickens were wanted and agree on the price before he killed any.

By 1945 two-thirds of all the farms of New Hampshire had telephones, giving the state sixth place in the nation in this respect.

Radio and the motion picture came to New Hampshire with the wider use of electricity. The first "wireless hams"—as radio enthusiasts were then called—began to appear in our state before the First World War. In 1920 broadcasting as we know it today started with KDKA in Pittsburgh. In 1922 New Hampshire had its own first radio station in Laconia. Ten years later there were similar stations in Manchester and Portsmouth. After that the growth of radio was rapid until almost every medium-sized town and city had a station of its own. The first small motion-picture theaters were opened in Concord and Manchester in 1906. In 1928 the first "talking moving pictures" were shown in the state, and movie attendance became extremely popular in the 1930s.

The better to promote business, the New England Council was formed in December, 1925, with New Hampshire men active in its list of original members. This council stimulated the formation in 1937 of the New England Governors' Conference, which sought to bring the six governors into cooperation on many matters.

In 1933 there began the development of six regional promotional areas in the state. These were the Monadnock Association, the White Mountain Association, the Seacoast Association, the Merrimack Valley Association, the Lakes Region Association, and the Dartmouth-Lake Sunapee Association. Each of these six regional groups had a salaried secretary to aid in the promotion of its interests, and each was supported by appropriations from its member towns and cities.

As in other states, successful businessmen in New Hampshire frequently made handsome gifts to the towns or cities in which they had been born or lived. Between 1886 and 1895 Austin Corbin of Newport developed the great game preserve in Croydon and Grantham which has always been called Corbin Park. Charles E. Tilton in the 1880s gave Tilton more than a hundred statues—five of which are still standing in 1964—and the monumental arch which dominates the near-by skyline. Frank P. Carpenter of Manchester gave his city the building for the Manchester Historic Association and also the public library. Moody Currier and Mrs. Emma Blood French, likewise of Manchester, presented to that city its Art Gallery and its Institute of Arts and Sciences. George A. and John S. Pillsbury, the flour millers, gave Sutton a town hall and Concord a hospital. Ambrose Swasey of Exeter presented to his town a beautiful parkway along the Squamscott River. John Shedd and Mrs. Jane A. Tracy gave their towns of Alstead and New London each a handsome library. Mrs. Robert P. Bass made possible the impressive building of the Peterborough Historical Society. In these ways the wealth of the business leadership of the state flowed back to benefit the people.

New Cities and New People

At the end of the Civil War there were just five cities in the state. In the period covered by this chapter, six more were incorporated: Keene in 1873, Rochester in 1891, Laconia and Somersworth in 1893, Franklin in 1894, and Berlin in 1897. The incorporation of Claremont in 1947 and of Lebanon in 1957 gave New Hampshire its present total of thirteen cities. As early as 1910, more than half the population of the state lived in these cities. By the end of the Second World War about fifty-six percent of all the people in New Hampshire were residents of what the U.S. census called "urban" areas.

As they grew, the cities had to grapple with many problems. It soon became necessary to pave the principal streets, and various materials were tried, including cobblestones, brick, granite blocks, asphalt, and finally concrete. More adequate water supplies became necessary, and city water systems were developed. Street lighting changed from gas to electricity after 1882. Better fire protection was eagerly sought, and new equipment was bought by many cities. In 1899 a Manchester citizen wrote proudly that his city had ". . . one of the finest, if not the very finest, fire departments in the world." City parks were started, such as the noted Greeley Park in Nashua and Langdon Park in Portsmouth. Many cities placed monuments in their principal squares, as did Manchester, with its statue of Abraham Lincoln by the sculptor John Rogers.

Into these thriving New Hampshire cities came a host of immigrants from Canada and from Europe. The number of French Canadians who reached New Hampshire from Quebec in the years between 1865 and 1945 was extraordinary. According to the U.S. census of 1870 there were then 5000 Franco-Americans within the state. Sixty years later the number had grown to 122,000. New Hampshire thus attained the distinction of having proportionately the largest number of French-Canadian people among its citizens of any state in the Union. The principal centers to which these Canadian immigrants came were Manchester, Nashua, Somersworth, Laconia, and Berlin.

Devoted to the Roman Catholic Church, the newcomers built institutions of that religious faith wherever they settled.

New hospitals, parochial schools, convents, houses of mercy, and even new banking institutions were founded. Many French newspapers were started in the state, some of them lasting for more than fifty years. The Canadians brought with them their love of snowshoeing, and clubs featuring this winter sport were started. In 1896 in Manchester the Association Canado-Americaine was founded; it sought to develop a library on French history, to build up insurance protection for the people, and to aid in the preservation of French culture.

Other thousands of immigrants arrived from Europe. Until 1882 most of these had come from northern European countries; after that year more came from southern and eastern European nations. By 1916 Manchester included foreign-born citizens from Ireland, Germany, Poland, Sweden, England, Scotland, Greece, Syria, Lithuania, Italy, Albania, Portugal, Russia, Norway, Armenia, Denmark, Belgium, Finland, Bulgaria, the Netherlands, Switzerland, and Spain. All these kinds of people in one New Hampshire city! Our other cities had similar types of newcomers. In some places there were even a few Chinese. By 1910 the number of foreign-born people in New Hampshire was almost twenty-five per cent of the entire population of the state.

Many interesting developments resulted from these new arrivals. The peoples from eastern Europe brought with them the Greek Orthodox faith, and soon their churches appeared in Manchester, Dover, Concord, Keene, and Nashua. Some of the new arrivals were Jews, and they built synagogues in Manchester, Concord, and Nashua. The Norwegians around Berlin introduced skiing into New Hampshire in 1872, giving the state its early leadership in the nation in this kind of sport. The Greeks and the Finns founded fraternal societies which have ever since flourished. The Germans started a new college in Manchester in 1889, giving it the name of St. Anselm's College. In these ways the life of our state was enriched and varied by contributions of new ideas and new customs from many lands.

As the number of workers in the cities increased, so also did their desire to form labor unions. By 1886 the number of union members in New Hampshire was such that several "strikes" for better working conditions took place. In 1893 the legislature created the Bureau of Labor. Its recommendations for better hours, wages, and working conditions came to be of ever greater influence in the thinking of the people. In 1901 the New Hampshire State Federation of Labor was established, shortly to affiliate with the American Federation of Labor. The next year the unions in the paper and wood-pulp industry of our state secured a contract agreement with their employers that was a model of its kind. Basic pay was then set at $1.25 a day, and ten hours a day was the normal working period.

The severe strikes of the 1920s and the difficulties of the depression years of the 1930s brought still further efforts to improve the lot of the city working people. In 1933 the legislature passed a minimum-wage law for women, setting this at fifty cents an hour. State inspection of factories was stiffened in 1935. Workmen's compensation laws were tightened in 1941 and again at the end of the Second World War. The new national labor organization called the CIO appeared in New Hampshire in 1937, and other national unions had some "locals" in the state. Although New Hampshire for the most part escaped the bitterness of labor strife which characterized so many cities just before the Second World War, it was familiar with the problems of laboring people and fully aware of their importance. Organized labor in our state served faithfully in both world wars and avoided strikes during the years of conflict.

The Developing Countryside

In the first years after 1865 it seemed as if rural life in New Hampshire was falling apart. Hundreds of farms were abandoned as the people set out for the new western states or for the cities to get jobs in the rising factories. In 1870 there were 2,334,487 acres of improved land in the state; by 1900 the amount of such land was just over a million acres. As a poetical writer in the 1890s put it:

> The woods are taking back these fields
> They lost two hundred years ago;
> White birch have surged across old walls,
> White pines are sowing a soft brown snow.
>
> When evening chill flows down the slope
> The groundhog creeps to earth, and soon
> Vague deer have vanished beyond the knoll
> Where thin slate tombstones face the moon.
>
> Then moonlight starts the quaver of owls
> And sobbing throb of whippoorwills;
> And there's whispering among the trees
> Over the fields lost in the hills.

But just when it seemed that New Hampshire farm life was drifting into hopeless decay, new forces appeared to revive and improve country living. One of these was the Grange, which entered the state at Exeter in August, 1873. This remarkable organization, officially styled The Patrons of Husbandry, had been founded in Washington in 1867. So fast did it grow that by 1890 there were a hundred Grange "locals" in our state. In 1920 more than 250 Granges in New Hampshire had a total membership in excess of 30,000. The Grange gave the farmers and other rural dwellers, both men and women, many kinds of information and helped them to express themselves and make their needs known.

Another factor that greatly helped country life was the efforts of the state and the federal governments. The New Hampshire Board of Agriculture had been started in 1871, and the U.S. government in 1887 began a series of laws to help farmers which have been increasing in significance ever since. Just before the First World War, cooperative extension programs sponsored by the U.S. Department of Agriculture began in New Hampshire. "County agents" became a part of the life of the state. The 4–H Clubs were first organized here in 1914; and the

Eastern States Exposition began at West Springfield, Massachusetts, in 1916. Meantime, under the terms of the Morrill Act of 1862, what is now called the University of New Hampshire had been started. This provided many courses to help the farmer.

A third force that improved New Hampshire farm life was the new emphasis on dairying. As Boston and the great cities in southern New England grew, there was an ever-increasing demand for milk. Special railroad cars and tank trucks were developed to carry milk in large quantities to the cities, and millions of gallons were shipped out each year. Butter and cheese production, too, increased greatly. By 1914 the total value of dairy products in New Hampshire was reckoned in the millions of dollars, and it has continued to grow ever since. There was a constant improvement in milk cows, and each of the state's principal breeds—Guernseys, Holsteins, Jerseys—had headquarters where lists of registered animals were kept. The legislature authorized measures to stamp out animal diseases and to require high standards in the production of pure milk products.

As the increase in dairy products gave new life to New Hampshire farm areas, so also did the rise of the poultry business. By the First World War the production of eggs in the state had more than doubled over what it had been at the ending of the Civil War, and it would double again before 1945. Meantime, many farmers began to raise chickens for the market. In the 1920s Professor A. W. Richardson of the University of New Hampshire developed a new breed of chickens called "New Hampshire Reds." By the end of the Second World War poultry was the largest single item in the agricultural income of our state. The annual gross income from chickens and eggs exceeded $30,000,000.

A fourth factor that aided the rural areas was the new interest which we call "conservation." Under this kind of planning, much land that was really not suitable for farming was purchased by the state or federal governments, or by private individuals, and turned back into forests. For example, Harvard and Yale and Dartmouth Colleges acquired large tracts of land on which all kinds of trees were raised. This strong desire to preserve the beauty of the countryside by maintaining forests was splendidly suggested by a poem published in 1914 by a young man who spent his summers on a farm near Swanzey. His name was Joyce Kilmer; his poem was called "Trees."

One great stimulus to rural New Hampshire was the new type of summer activities that developed from the influx of summer visitors. "Summer boarders" had been coming ever since the 1840s, but in the 1880s and thereafter the number greatly increased. In 1913 a New Hampshire official noted that the state was fast becoming the pleasure ground of a large proportion of the people of the United States. As a result, more and more farms were turned into summer residences or permanent homes. Cottages encircled the many inviting lakes in the state, and it was estimated that—at that early date— more than $50,000,000 was invested in summer vacation facilities. The summer visitors meant also, of course, a larger market for farm and dairy products so that "a large part of the fruit, vegetables, meat, eggs, and poultry consumed by these guests has to be shipped back to the country from the large wholesale markets in our cities."

Another new summer activity in the state was the summer-camp movement. The first organized summer camp for boys in the United States was started on Squam Lake in 1881 by a man named Ernest Balch. By 1945 there were more than 200 camps in New Hampshire, capable of taking care of more than 20,000 young people.

And last of all it may be noted that the sport of golf came into New Hampshire in the late 1890s. To build the extensive courses, much farm land was acquired and expensively improved. This process began in Concord with the Beaver Meadow Country Club in 1897. Fifty years later there were more than seventy golf courses dotted all over the state. Describing the first golf courses as they were built about 1900, L. H. Dowling wrote in 1952:[11]

The courses of that day? Well, they were crude affairs as compared with today's beautiful layouts, grass tees, well-kept fairways, and manicured greens. Then, we used sand to tee up a ball. On rainy days—and when did rain ever halt a real golfer?—it was quite a feat to play the stroke before the tee was washed away! Many courses of the long ago treated themselves to fenced-in greens, and it was a common sight to find cattle grazing on the fairways.

[11] *See Bibliography referring to Chapter 10.*

11. *An Expansion of Mind and Spirit*
1865–1945

In 1862 Congress passed the famous Morrill Act, the law which made extensive land grants to the states to assist them in providing colleges for their young people. New Hampshire accepted the terms of this grant—which in our case amounted to 150,000 acres of land in Wisconsin—and decided to locate the new college in Hanover. It was to be operated there in conjunction with Dartmouth and was to specialize in agriculture and mechanic arts. Under President Ezekiel Dimond, the college opened at Hanover on April 28, 1868. The total attendance in any one year while the college was situated there varied between ten and fifty, and the largest graduating class was fourteen in 1881.

On January 30, 1890, Benjamin Thompson of Durham

died. In his will he directed that the major portion of his land and property be left to the state of New Hampshire. This was on condition that there be located a state-supported agricultural college in the town of Durham. A year later the legislature accepted the terms and authorized the removal of the New Hampshire College of Agriculture and Mechanic Arts from Hanover to Durham. During the summer of 1893 the equipment and books of the institution were taken from Hanover to the new campus at Durham, and the state college opened in its present location in September. First president of the newly removed college was Charles S. Murkland of Manchester. Ten years later when Murkland resigned his post, the New Hampshire College of Agriculture and Mechanic Arts had grown to 185 students. In another ten years the enrollment had increased to 315.

In 1917 the college came under the leadership of President Ralph D. Hetzel. Dr. Hetzel was determined that the institution should have a more active part in the life of the state. He persuaded the lawmakers to grant greatly increased financial support, and in 1923 he secured legislative permission to change the name to the University of New Hampshire. The new title went into effect on July 1 of that year. Since that date, the University of New Hampshire has steadily grown in size and importance until it is today one of the fine land-grant colleges of the sixty-eight in the United States.

While New Hampshire was slowly developing its state university, it saw also the rise of other collegiate institutions. In 1871 the legislature authorized the founding of a state normal school at Plymouth, and in 1909 a similar institution was started at Keene. In 1939 both these normal schools were permitted to take the title of Teachers College. In 1889 St. Anselm's College was founded in Manchester; it actually opened in 1893. In 1928 Colby Junior College for Women replaced the historic Colby Academy in New London. Mount Saint Mary College at Hooksett was begun in 1934 and the very next year Rivier College at Nashua opened its doors. Both these last-named were for women. In 1946, just after the end of the Second World War, New England College, a coeducational institution, was started at Henniker.

Meanwhile, Dartmouth College underwent expansion. The Thayer School of Engineering and the Tuck School of Administration and Finance were opened. Intercollegiate athletics began, as did the fraternity system. The Dartmouth Outing Club was founded in 1909, and the first winter carnival was held two years later. In 1916 President Ernest M. Hopkins began his notable term as head of Dartmouth. He tremendously stimulated alumni support and was responsible for many of the present college buildings. For example, he dedicated the Baker Library in 1928. Closely related to Dartmouth was the great Hitchcock Clinic, organized at Hanover in 1927 by two Dartmouth alumni, Dr. John F. Gile and Dr. John Bowler.

New Hampshire elementary and secondary schools also developed rapidly. As the public high schools became ever more numerous, the old and many new private academies continued their useful work. Exeter Academy observed its centennial in 1883. Holderness School began in 1879, and St. Mary's in the Mountains opened its doors in Bethlehem in 1936. The Brewster Free Academy at Wolfeboro was started in 1887. Roman Catholic parochial schools appeared in every large place where members of that church were numerous.

In 1919 an outstanding change took place in the public educational system of New Hampshire when a complete reorganization was effected by state law. Under this program, so-called "supervisory unions" were established; a State Board of Education was begun; the office of State Commissioner of Education was instituted; and rules on the certification of teachers were stiffened.

New Hampshire has developed an excellent system of public schools and furnished many noted teachers to the nation. The first president of Wellesley College, founded in Massachusetts in 1875, was Ada Lydia Howard, a native of Temple. Katherine A. Sanborn, born in Hanover, taught in several colleges, including Smith, and wrote popular books. Elisha B. Andrews, a native of Hinsdale, was president of Brown University for a time; and Francis Wayland Parker, born in Bedford, was the first head of the School of Education at the University of Chicago. The New Hampshire Congress of Parents and Teachers, generally known as the P.T.A., was started in 1913. The New Hampshire State Library system of "bookmobiles," which provide books to thousands of readers in villages and towns in the state, began in 1938.

The Professions, Sciences, and the Fine Arts

The whole development of hospitals in the modern sense of that term took place after 1865. The first such institution in our state had been the state hospital in Concord, which opened in 1842. In 1881 the Elliott Hospital in Manchester opened, followed closely by similar hospitals in all the principal cities and towns of the state. The first New Hampshire state examinations for the coveted title of Registered Nurse were held in 1910. The State Board of Health was begun in 1881, the Dental Board in 1891, and the Board of Optometry in 1911. The state sanitarium at Glencliff was started in 1916. Because it was not equipped to operate a four-year advanced course, Dartmouth Medical School founded in 1798 ceased conferring the M.D. degree in 1914. Blue Cross began in New Hampshire in 1942; the Blue Shield was added in 1944.

In the legal profession New Hampshire produced an outstanding Chief Justice of the State Supreme Court. This was Charles Doe, who served in this post from 1876 to 1896. His pioneering work in the relation of law to problems of psychiatry has never been forgotten. In 1925 President Coolidge appointed Harlan Fiske Stone, a native of Chesterfield, New Hampshire, to be an Associate Justice of the U.S. Supreme Court; in 1941 Stone became Chief Justice, the second New Hampshire-born man ever to hold this high post. Stone was one of four New Hampshire natives to serve on the U.S.

Supreme Court; the previous appointees had been Levi Woodbury, Nathan Clifford, and Salmon P. Chase.

Noteworthy New Hampshire scientists during these years included Gordon F. Hull and E. F. Nichols of Dartmouth, who helped lay the foundations on which modern physics rests. Their experiments in the nature of light became world-famous. John R. Eastman of Andover was an outstanding astronomer; Warren Upham of Amherst was a noted geologist; and Charles G. Abbot of Wilton served for years as secretary of the Smithsonian Institution in Washington. Beginning in 1932, a group of New Hampshire scientists undertook systematic daily weather observations on the top of Mount Washington. These observers on April 12, 1934, recorded the greatest wind velocity ever measured anywhere on earth: 231 miles an hour!

In 1907 the American musician Edward MacDowell and his wife, Marian N. MacDowell, founded near Peterborough what has ever since been known as the MacDowell Colony. Here practitioners of the fine arts have found a haven of peace and quiet for all the years that followed. Between 1865 and 1945, seventeen Pulitzer Prize winners in literature or music did creative work in this place. Among these were Edwin Arlington Robinson, Willa Cather, Stephen Vincent Benét, Thornton Wilder, William Rose Benét, and Aaron Copland. Willa Cather, the novelist, so fell in love with New Hampshire during her stay at the MacDowell Colony and later at Jaffrey that in 1947 she provided in her will for burial in the hilltop cemetery in the latter town. As a result of the tremendous stimulus to the fine arts given by the MacDowell Colony, the New Hampshire Federation of Music Clubs was established in 1909. Nor should it be forgotten that the popular song of the First World War, "There's a Long Long Trail A-Winding," was written in 1913 by Alonzo Elliott of Manchester.

Between 1900 and 1915 Winston Churchill at his home in Cornish wrote many of his most famous novels: *The Crisis, Coniston, Mr. Crewe's Career, The Inside of the Cup.* Thornton Wilder wrote the play *Our Town* in 1938, describing Grover's Corners, a mythical New Hampshire village. Robert Frost, who lived in New Hampshire for much of his life, wrote his early books of poetry—*North of Boston, West-Running Brook*, and others—with a New Hampshire setting. In 1937 Stephen Vincent Benét was the author of *The Devil and Daniel Webster*, laid in a New Hampshire town. Donald C. Babcock of the University of New Hampshire faculty wrote varied and charming poetry. In 1931 Thomas C. Dreier, working for the New Hampshire State Development Commission, began the monthly magazine called *The Troubadour*. Typical of the many lovely poems that appeared in this publication until its discontinuance in 1951 was one by Mary C. Davies in March, 1932:

> *They dream of farms, those city folk,*
> *Who know the great towns' heavy yoke,*
> *Who on their flesh feel every stroke*
>   *Of trade's unflagging whips;*
> *They dream of farms and maple trees,*
> *Of clover fields and drowsy bees,*
> *As those sad exiles far from seas*
>   *Dream still of ships.*
>
> *They dream of farms, of soil and sod*
> *Where their forefathers, farmers, trod*
> *And shared the mystery with God*
>   *Of giving green things birth.*
> *They long to leave the city shrill,*
> *Where souls are ground in greed's great mill,*
> *They want to find and own and till*
>   *Their share of earth.*
>
> *And we who long have had in fee*
> *What they so yearn for ceaselessly,*
> *We hold our treasure carelessly,*
>   *And even half despise*
> *These fields, a too familiar sight,*
> *The little farmhouse warm with light*
> *That seems, to hosts who dream tonight,*
>   *A paradise.*

The pictorial and graphic arts also found expression in New Hampshire during this period. In 1885 the brilliant American sculptor, Augustus St. Gaudens, came to Cornish and set up his studio. Here he completed the superb statue of Abraham Lincoln which today stands in Lincoln Park, Chicago; and here also he sculptured the statue of the Puritan which stands in Springfield, Massachusetts. Another great sculptor, Daniel French, came from Exeter. His figure of the Minuteman at Concord Bridge in Massachusetts was the first of an unforgettable series of famous works of art; and his majestic statue of Abraham Lincoln in the Lincoln Memorial at Washington fittingly closed his artistic career. Near Dublin lived the strange and shy genius, Abbott Thayer, who became known as the "Father of Camouflage." Thayer's studies in the artistry of bird coloration have been summarized as Thayer's Law and are formulated in his book, *Concealing Coloration in the Animal Kingdom* (1909). Ralph Adams Cram, a notable architect of the period, was a native of Hampton.

The American theater was enriched by the work of several New Hampshire men. Denman Thompson, who grew up in Swanzey, was the author of *The Old Homestead,* an immensely popular play which went on a national tour as early as 1885 and has been revived every year since 1942 at the Potash Bowl in Swanzey. Charles H. Hoyt of Charlestown, through his play, *Temperance Town,* made this community famous. Benjamin F. Keith of Hillsborough became a nationally known owner of theaters. His aim was to provide a chain of such theaters as would offer "refined entertainment for the public, and high standards of vaudeville." In this effort he largely succeeded, for at his death in 1914 he owned more than 400 theaters from coast to coast.

Many Expressions of Religion

The churches which were flourishing in New Hampshire at the end of the Civil War continued to be active during the next eight decades. The Protestant denominations and the Roman Catholic faith grew steadily in membership as the state's population increased. Meanwhile, the great religious currents which were moving among the American people manifested themselves in New Hampshire also. The work of such popular revivalists as Dwight L. Moody and Ira D. Sankey was much admired in our state. In 1877 and again in 1896 these two famous men spoke in Manchester, attracting thousands of listeners. The New Hampshire Bible Society continued its useful work in the area of home missions and observed its centennial in 1912. The Society of Christian Endeavor, founded by the Reverend Francis E. Clark of Claremont, came to our state in 1882, while The International Order of the King's Daughters and Sons started its first chapter in New Hampshire in 1888.

New religious faiths became strong during this eighty-year period. As mentioned in the previous chapter, the first Jewish congregation was organized in Manchester in 1892 and built its own synagogue in 1911. The first Greek Orthodox Church was founded in Manchester in 1905. In 1886 the National Christian Science Association was formed. This was the result of the thinking of a remarkable woman born in Bow, New Hampshire, in 1821, and best known by her married name of Mary Baker Eddy. Mrs. Eddy lived in New Hampshire from 1889 to 1908 and was the leader of the Christian Science Church during all that period. She was generous in her gifts to her native state and left behind at her death in 1910 a strong following, not only in New Hampshire but in many parts of the world. Her portrait hangs today in the State House in Concord.

Other new manifestations of organized religion appeared in the state. For example, the Salvation Army first entered New Hampshire in 1886. The summer-camp movement of the Y.M.C.A. began with the "Y" camp on Lake Winnipesaukee in 1903, to be followed shortly by many similar camps all over the state. On Star Island in the Isles of Shoals, religious gatherings were held each summer. "Spiritualist" associations were numerous in the state in the 1880s and 1890s. Russell Durgin of Concord, a graduate of Dartmouth College in the class of 1915, went to Japan to become head of the Y.M.C.A. in that country, and to remain there until 1941. Several hymn writers—Jeremiah E. Rankin, John Henry Gilmore, and O. S. Davis—had connections with our state during these years.

In 1927 the LaSalette Fathers, a missionary order of the Roman Catholic Church, purchased the property of the one-time Shaker Colony at Enfield. This handsome group of buildings set upon 1100 acres of land furnished an excellent site for a new seminary of that order. In connection with the LaSalette seminary, the members soon developed a shrine which in the years after the Second World War attracted thousands of visitors to the state.

Another great religious shrine which was founded in New Hampshire at the very end of the period was the Cathedral of the Pines at Rindge. It was established in memory of Lieutenant Sanderson Sloane, a summer resident of Rindge, who, with all aboard his B-17 airplane, was killed in action over Germany on February 22, 1944. At the center of the Cathedral of the Pines is the Altar of the Nation, composed of stones from all the states of the United States and from many foreign nations. Of this shrine it has been written:

The Cathedral of the Pines is dedicated to the Glory of God and was given in loving and grateful memory of Sanderson Sloane by his parents, Douglas and Sibyl Sanderson Sloane, as a place where all people may come and worship, each in his own way, returning thanks to Almighty God for His innumerable benefits, for the strength and inspiration which come from His hills, solace and assurance from His valleys with their lifegiving waters, joy from the songs of His birds, courage, under God's boundless heaven, to meet the daily needs, sympathy and understanding by association one with the other, and as the wind whispers through His Pines, re-echoing voices and prayers from the past, acknowledge, each for himself, a continuing obligation to the forefathers to keep secure their heritage of spiritual and intellectual freedoms.

OTHER VARIETIES OF SOCIAL GROWTH AND CHANGE

A new idea of great importance to the rural dwellers of New Hampshire, as elsewhere in the nation, was the beginning of Rural Free Delivery, better known as R.F.D., in 1896. In that year Congress, after much debate, authorized this new concept of mail service. In New Hampshire within a few years there was a network of mail routes scattered all over the state. Prior to this system the farmer's mail might have stayed in the town post office for days or even weeks until he found time to collect it. Now it was possible for him to receive it daily, with great and beneficial consequences. After 1912, Congress added such services as parcel post and postal savings, further aids to the citizen who lived far from urban communities.

Perhaps as a partial result of this method of bringing people together, the observance of New Hampshire Old Home Week began. At a meeting held in the State House in June, 1899, Governor Frank W. Rollins proposed the annual observance of an Old Home Week in the third week of August. The program captured the imagination of many people, and each summer since scores of towns and cities celebrate the week. In 1913 the legislature formally endorsed the idea by passing an appropriate law. In 1933 a bronze tablet commemorating Governor Rollins and the establishment of Old Home Week was dedicated in the same room in the State House where the project had originated.

This interest in history, evidenced by the celebrations of Old Home Week, was shown in many other ways. Four statues were placed on the plaza in front of the State House in memory of four of New Hampshire's famous sons: Daniel Webster in 1886, John Stark in 1890, John P. Hale in 1892, and Franklin Pierce in 1914. New Hampshire paid further tribute to Daniel Webster by giving a principal highway his name. In 1923 there were elaborate ceremonies in honor of the 300th birthday of the state. In 1938 New Hampshire fittingly commemorated its part in the 150th anniversary of the formation of the United States Constitution.

Efforts to bring greater help to the unfortunate members of society were numerous. The New Hampshire Conference on Social Welfare was organized in 1898, seeking to correlate the many kinds of voluntary services which were developing. In 1912 the New Hampshire Association for the Blind began its long and useful service to persons thus afflicted. The first Community Chest organization appeared in our state shortly after the First World War. Beginning in 1916, the New Hampshire Tuberculosis Association sponsored the sale of Christmas seals each year to fight that disease. In 1935 the annual sale of Easter seals for work with crippled children began. The first Boy Scout troop was organized in our state in 1912, and the first Girl Scout unit came two years later.

Adult organizations brought people from all parts of the state more closely together. The New Hampshire Federation of Women's Clubs was organized in 1895. Forty years later there were more than 14,000 women included in 175 clubs, both senior and junior, scattered all over the state. The League of Women Voters was started in New Hampshire in 1920, and the New Hampshire Federation of Business and Professional Women's Clubs in 1924. The first Rotary Club in our state was founded in Manchester in 1918, and shortly thereafter many other men's service clubs were started. The Junior Chamber of Commerce appeared in New Hampshire in the 1930s.

Modern Americans come together for recreation and for organized sport in many areas of activity. For example, the summer-theater movement began in this state in the early 1930s, with several companies putting on performances during the months of July and August. Large-scale winter sports began in New Hampshire in 1931 when the first "snow trains" for skiers ran from Boston to Warner. The first ski lift in the

United States was opened in Vermont in the winter of 1933–1934, but New Hampshire soon built many such devices of its own. In 1937–1938 the state-owned and operated Cannon Mountain Aerial Tramway began operations. A second state-owned chairlift development was authorized by the legislature of 1941, to be built on Mount Sunapee. Owing to the interruption of the Second World War, however, this was not actually finished until 1948.

In all these ways the people of New Hampshire during the eighty years from 1865 to 1945 expanded old institutions and made new ones. By the end of the Second World War it is safe to say that all our citizens were more closely tied together in mind and spirit than they had ever been in the past. In daily life there were few things a person could do that were not closely related to the activities of others.

12. *New Hampshire in the Space Age*

As was true everywhere in the Western world, the basic characteristic of life in New Hampshire during the years after 1945 was a continuous series of changes in the direction of interdependence. With ever greater speed the last vestiges of self-sufficiency disappeared from our common life, and more and more we were tied into the main stream of civilization.

After the Second World War New Hampshire saw much reordering of its public institutions. This was a pattern common to many of the states. For example, between 1949 and 1953 Governor Sherman Adams, seeking greater efficiency and "streamlining," pushed through a far-reaching program of reorganization of state government. Just ten years later, between 1959 and 1963, Governor Wesley Powell likewise sponsored an elaborate reorganization of state government. While these two energetic governors made relatively extensive innovations, many critics demanded still further modifications of existing patterns. Some felt that the old-fashioned system of county organization should be abandoned completely in New Hampshire, as it had been in Connecticut. Others, including Governor John W. King in 1963, urged that the municipal courts of the state be drastically revised. Still others insisted that New Hampshire should enact a general sales tax, or a graduated income tax, the better to support the work of state government.

The highway system of the state after 1945 saw great developments. Modern expressways—four-lane, divided roads, with limited access—came to New Hampshire with the completion of the New Hampshire Turnpike along the seacoast in 1949. There followed the opening of the first section of the Everett Turnpike in the Merrimack Valley in 1955, and the building of the Spaulding Turnpike near Rochester in 1957. A fine new road called the Kancamagus Highway was constructed across the wildest part of the White Mountain area in the early 1960s, connecting Lincoln with North Conway. After the passage of the U.S. Interstate Highway Act of 1956, many miles of the new Interstate System were built and projected in the state, notably the Styles Bridges Highway north of Concord.

The better to assist postwar business activities in New Hampshire, the legislature in 1951 authorized the formation of the New Hampshire Business Development Corporation. This semi-public corporation sought to secure new businesses for New Hampshire and to encourage older establishments to embark upon modernization programs. In 1955 the legislature approved the establishment of an Industrial Park Authority to increase this kind of promotional work. Not necessarily related to this effort was the remarkable rise of the miniature precision ball-bearing industry in New Hampshire, with large plants located at such places as Keene, Lebanon, and Peterborough.

The same trend toward working more closely together was manifest in many ways other than public life and business.

The New Hampshire Council of Churches was formed in 1945 to bring together the chief Protestant faiths of the state for mutual help and cooperation. Special study groups were launched to consider the problem of geriatrics—the needs of the aged. According to figures gathered in 1952, New Hampshire had then the largest proportion of people above the age of sixty-five years of any state in the nation. School districts were encouraged to unite in "regional" building programs, and many such enlarged districts were authorized by the voters; among these were consolidated schools in Moultonborough and Durham.

Educational facilities were augmented throughout the state. In 1946 a new preparatory school for boys named the Cardigan Mountain School was started at Canaan. Ten years later the College of Advanced Science was founded in the same place. Notre Dame College for women started at Manchester in 1950. Community colleges in Lebanon and Peterborough were begun in 1957. In 1962 Nathaniel Hawthorne College opened at Antrim. Initiated for 1963 were three new colleges: Franklin Pierce College at Rindge, Franconia Junior College at Franconia, and Belknap College at Moultonborough. The facilities of the University of New Hampshire and of the state colleges at Plymouth and at Keene were well coordinated. Dartmouth College made many experiments in curriculum and in teaching method and attracted students to its campus from every state in the union.

The innovation of TV had great impact upon life in New Hampshire. Until 1956 the people of the state were dependent on stations situated outside our borders. But in that year two New Hampshire TV stations opened, one in Manchester, the other on top of Mount Washington. From these two outlets most of the homes and schools in the state were covered. Then, in 1959, an educational television channel, Channel 11 at Durham, was organized. Much of the state was within reach of this outlet, and excellent educational programs were telecast from its transmitter. For example, the study of New Hampshire history, a required subject in the fourth grade, was greatly stimulated by a TV course developed for Channel 11 by Mrs. Dorothy Wilcox of Durham.

New Hampshire within the United States

On the governmental level New Hampshire had ever closer relationships with the federal authorities in Washington. In 1958 Governor Lane Dwinell served as co-chairman of a national committee to study the puzzling question of the proper relationships between the states and the nation. He found that at that time there were fifty-two federal-aid programs from which New Hampshire could benefit in six major areas: old-age assistance, highway construction, school-lunch programs, school operations and school construction in certain places, employment security, and hospital construction. Many of these were of such obvious help to the people of the state that they were gladly accepted. U.S.-supported flood-control projects were popular in New Hampshire as in other places in New England. In 1959 Vice-President Richard M. Nixon came to our state to initiate construction on a huge flood-control dam near Hopkinton. In 1956 Congressman Chester Merrow co-sponsored a federal law to give aid to small rural libraries in towns of under 10,000 population. But still the argument continued: How much federal aid and for what purpose?

In 1908 the so-called Governors' Conferences, annual meetings of all the state governors in the United States, had begun. In 1949 Governor Charles M. Dale had the pleasure of being host to the Governors' Conference of that year, held at Portsmouth. In 1962 Governor Wesley Powell served as chairman of the Governors' Conference held in Pennsylvania. Along somewhat similar lines, New Hampshire was represented at the White House Conference on Children and Youth held in 1950 and at the White House Conference on Education five years later.

Many New Hampshire people played active parts on the

national stage. In 1946 at the official memorial service for the late President Franklin D. Roosevelt, held in Washington, former Governor John G. Winant gave the principal address. New Hampshire's long-time Senator Styles Bridges won for himself a place of power in the national capital until his death in 1961. U.S. Senator Norris Cotton carried many responsibilities, including membership on the Commission on Government Security in 1956. Congressman Chester Merrow helped to set up the United Nations Educational, Scientific and Cultural Organization (UNESCO) at a meeting in London in 1945.

Because of the timing of our presidential primary election, New Hampshire is the first state to choose its delegates to the national party conventions in a presidential election year. In 1952 Governor Sherman Adams was one of the leaders in the movement to nominate General Dwight D. Eisenhower for the presidency. In a spectacular campaign in New Hampshire in March the Eisenhower slate was elected, and Eisenhower went on from this auspicious start to win the presidency in November. He promptly named Governor Adams as Assistant to the President. Adams held this post until 1958 when he resigned his high office. While he was in this position he twice arranged for President Eisenhower to visit New Hampshire, once in 1953 and again in 1955. On the first visit Eisenhower received an honorary degree from Dartmouth College.

Turning to other aspects of our state's relation to the nation, it may be noted that twice during the years after the Second World War, the General Federation of Women's Clubs elected a New Hampshire woman as its president: Mrs. LaFell Dickinson of Keene in 1945–1946, and Mrs. Dexter Arnold in 1962–1963. In 1946 and 1947 New Hampshire women won the national essay contest co-sponsored by the General Federation of Women's Clubs and the *Atlantic Monthly*. In 1948 the book *Lost Boundaries,* laid in New Hampshire, became a best-seller. It was later made into a motion picture, filmed in New Hampshire with a local cast.

Many national movements came to New Hampshire during

this postwar period. In 1946 the National Farm Bureau instituted the practice in our state of naming a Mother of the Year, and this high award has been granted annually since that time. In 1947 the Gordon Research Conferences, a division of the American Association for the Advancement of Science, came to this state for their summer assemblies. Meeting first in New London on the campus of Colby Junior College, they later expanded their offerings to include work at the New Hampton School and at Kimball Union Academy at Meriden. The noted American financial expert, Roger W. Babson, started his Gravity Research Center in 1948 at New Boston. In 1951 Norman Vincent Peale brought his "Guideposts" movement to New Hampshire. Before his death in 1962, the famous Arctic explorer Vilhjalmur Stefansson gave his unrivaled library to Dartmouth College, making that place a center for Arctic studies.

In matters of health, New Hampshire had a national reputation. For example, in 1946 a group of New Hampshire men led by Harry A. Gregg of Nashua planned a rehabilitation center for handicapped children in this state. By 1955 on a 1000-acre site near Greenfield, New Hampshire, a magnificent set of buildings had been erected and a fine medical staff acquired. It soon became nationally known for its work. As Dr. Howard A. Rusk of New York wrote in 1955:

Situated on a plateau of the mountain for which it is named, the Crotched Mountain Rehabilitation Center is unusual in two ways: it is the first rural rehabilitation center in the nation; and when current plans are fully implemented, it will be the most complete rehabilitation center not only in the United States, but probably in the world . . .

The first two units, which are now in operation, are the $2,000,000 Children's Center and the Catherwood Physical Medicine Wing. Built to accommodate 100 handicapped youngsters, the Children's Center now operates forty beds and provides a complete program of general and specialized medical services, physical therapy, occupational therapy, speech therapy, nursing care, psychological services, recreation and education.

Mary Beard, a famous registered nurse from Dover, was president of the National Organization for Public Health Nursing until her death in 1946.

New Hampshire in World Affairs

The outbreak of the war in Korea in June, 1950, affected New Hampshire in many ways. More than 8000 of the young men of the state at one time or another saw service in that conflict in East Asia. Two New Hampshire men in the Air Force achieved unusual repute: Colonel Harrison S. Thyng of Pittsfield and Captain Joseph McConnell of Portsmouth. The latter became the first "triple ace" of the Air Force in the Korean War.

In 1952 Operation Skywatch began. Manchester was the center for 368 observation posts scattered throughout New England; ninety-eight of these were manned twenty-four hours a day. The purpose was to detect and report every airplane in the sky. Hundreds of volunteers served in these observation posts, and their work was praised by the Air Force leadership. Following the armistice of July, 1953, these observation activities were discontinued.

Shortly after fighting broke out in Korea, the U.S. Strategic Air Command determined to build a large air base in New Hampshire for its newest jet bombers. Construction formally began in 1954. The new field was named Pease Air Force Base in honor of one of New Hampshire's heroes of the Second World War. Dedicated in September, 1957, it is located in the town of Newington, not far from Portsmouth, and is an integral part of the 8th Air Force of SAC. Its massive runways are more than two miles long, and its huge hangars accommodate two wings of jet planes. About 7000 men were assigned to the base, and its operations in times of crisis, as in the days of the

Cuban affair in October, 1962, are at a high state of readiness.

In 1954 Governor Hugh Gregg set aside Sunday, June 13, as Freedom Day in memory of those in East Berlin who a year before had revolted against their Communist masters. The governor called upon the people of New Hampshire to remember and pray for all those throughout the Soviet Empire who had fought and died for freedom. He reminded the people of the state of their own motto written for them by General John Stark, the victor of the Battle of Bennington in 1777, "Live Free or Die." In accord with this feeling for the victims of Communist oppression, New Hampshire assumed responsibility for a certain share of the refugees admitted under the provisions of the Congressional Displaced Persons Act of 1948, and under similar legislation enacted after the Hungarian uprising in 1956. In 1963 New Hampshire people likewise assumed responsibility for many refugees from Castro's Cuba.

In other ways New Hampshire manifested concern for world affairs. A factory in the state produced the wire for the first transatlantic telephone cables. Telegraphic cables, of course, were an old story, going back almost a century. But in 1955 the first of the new type of telephonic cable was laid across the Atlantic. In 1956 a second cable was laid, and in 1961 the third was put down. The last was the most complex of the three, having facilities for sixty circuits of two-way operations. Business activities like this accounted for the more than $50,000,000 worth of exports from New Hampshire to foreign markets each year in the 1960s.

New Hampshire sportsmen took an active part in world competitions. Athletes from the state, both men and women, entered each session of the Olympic Games—Helsinki in 1952, Melbourne in 1956, Rome in 1960. In 1953 two men from Exeter, Charles S. Houston and Robert H. Bates, led an expedition to ascend the second highest mountain in the world, the so-called K-2 in the Himalayas in Central Asia. Two years later, in Chile, Ralph Miller of Hanover achieved a world's speed record on skis by going down a measured slope in the Andes at an average rate of 109 miles an hour.

In May, 1961, the world was thrilled to learn that Commander Alan Shepard of East Derry was the first American astronaut to travel through outer space. His rocket-powered flight in a space capsule sent aloft from Cape Canaveral, Florida, was the beginning of a series of such flights that electrified the nation and the world in the months which followed. Commander Shepard visited New Hampshire later in 1961 and was given a great ovation by the people of his home town and the state in general. An oil painting of him in his space uniform now hangs in the State Capitol at Concord.

In 1958 a long series of repairs on "The Old Man of the Mountain" were completed. As early as 1875 mountain climbers had reported that the famous profile was in danger of breaking up due to the action of winter snows and frosts. Several efforts had been made to save the celebrated stone face. In 1958 major repairs were made and the "Old Man" faced ahead with renewed strength for the future. It was a happy augury for the state as a whole, and its part in the nation and in the world. Battered and somewhat fatigued by the pressures of modern living, New Hampshire still had strength and sturdiness with which to face the future of an atomic age. It was ready to play its part in the events to come in the same vigorous way which had always characterized it in the past.

Appendix A

Some Facts About New Hampshire

Nickname: The Granite State
Capitol City: Concord
Area: 9341 square miles
Population: 606,921 (1960)
Motto: "Live Free or Die"
Flower: Purple lilac
Tree: White birch
Bird: Purple finch
New Hampshire is the ninth of the Original Thirteen States.

NEW HAMPSHIRE STATE PARKS AND FORESTS

CRAWFORD NOTCH STATE PARK, Bartlett, N.H. (U.S. Route 302) Glacial trough, falls, native wildlife. Open May 30 to mid-October.

DIXVILLE NOTCH, Colebrook, N.H. (Route 26 between Colebrook and Errol) Sheer rock prominences rise spectacularly on both sides of highway.

FRANCONIA NOTCH STATE PARK, Echo Lake. (U.S. Route 3) Glacier-formed Old Man of the Mountain. Flume. Half-mile scenic walk through geologic chasm nearly 800 feet long. Open May 30 to mid-October.

CATHEDRAL LEDGE, North Conway. Views of structure of White Mountains from granite outcrop.

WHITE MOUNTAIN NATIONAL FOREST, Laconia, N.H. Mount Washington is the highest peak in northeastern United States, 6288 feet above sea level.

MONADNOCK STATE PARK, Jaffrey, N.H. Mount Monadnock rises 3165 feet above sea level, and on a clear day offers a spectacular view and picture of the geological structure of New England.

RHODODENDRON STATE RESERVATION, Fitzwilliam, N.H. Hemlock forest. Excellent views of Mount Monadnock.

MOUNT PROSPECT STATE PARK, Lancaster, N.H. Scenic mountain-top estate of John W. Weeks, a former Secretary of War. Open June to October.

MOUNT PAWTUCKAWAY STATE RESERVATION, Deerfield, N.H. Mountain rises 1011 feet above sea level. Extensive oak-hickory forest, hemlock ravine.

LOST RIVER RESERVATION, North Woodstock, N.H. (Route 112 from U.S. Route 3 at N. Woodstock or U.S. Route 302 at Woodsville) Paradise Falls, Giant Pothole.

KINSMAN NOTCH, North Woodstock, N.H. Deep gorge. A lost river winds through caverns and emerges in falls. Glacier-formed caves.

THATCHER FOREST, Hancock, N.H. Primeval white pine.

WINSLOW STATE PARK, Merrimack County. Mount Kearsarge forests.

MOUNT SUNAPEE STATE PARK (off Route 103, Newbury, N.H.) Open May 30 to mid-October and ski season.

MUSEUMS AND HISTORIC SITES

CLARKE HOUSE & OLD SCHOOLHOUSE EARLY AMERICAN LIVING MUSEUM, Wolfeboro, N.H. (Route 28) Open July 1–September 7.

DARTMOUTH COLLEGE MUSEUM, Hanover, N.H. Open all year.

EXETER HISTORIC HOUSES, Exeter, N.H. Ladd-Gilman House, 1721. Open mid-April to mid-October. Garrison House, c. 1650 and 1750. Open May 1 to November 1.

JOHN GOFFE'S MILL, WAYFARER MOTOR INN, Bedford, N.H. Many of original pieces of equipment operated by water power intact.

LIBBY MUSEUM, Wolfeboro, N.H. (Route 109) Natural history, and special art exhibits. Open June 25 to Labor Day.

MANCHESTER HISTORIC ASSOCIATION, 219 Amherst St., Manchester, N.H. Open all year.

MEREDITH AUTO MUSEUM, Route 3, Meredith, N.H. Open June 25 to September 9 and weekends in September.

MERIDEN BIRD MUSEUM & SANCTUARY, Meriden, N.H. Open July 1 to August 31.

MORSE MUSEUM, Warren, N.H. Collections of mounted animals, weapons, trophies and curios from all over the world. Open mid-May to mid-October.

MUSEUM OF OLD DOLLS AND TOYS, Chesterfield, N.H. Open Memorial Day to Columbus Day weekend.

MUSEUM OF SHAKER INVENTIONS & HANDICRAFTS, Canterbury, N.H. Shaker

Colony. (12 miles NE of Concord, Route 106). Open June 1 to October 12, except Sunday and Monday.

NEW HAMPSHIRE HISTORICAL SOCIETY AND LIBRARY, 30 Park Street, Concord, N.H. N.H. in Colonial period; paintings by G.P.A. Healy of Nathaniel Hawthorne, Franklin Pierce and Daniel Webster. Open all year.

OCEAN-BORN MARY HOUSE. Off Route 9 between Henniker and Hillsboro, N.H. Old Colonial home inspired ghost tales and the book by Lois Lenski, *Ocean-Born Mary*.

OLD STORE MUSEUM, So. Sutton, N.H.

PHILLIPS MUSEUM OF NATURAL HISTORY, Litchfield, N.H. Route 102. Birds, animals, fish.

SAINT-GAUDENS MEMORIAL, Cornish, N.H. On Route 12A. Home, studio, and work of the famous sculptor. Open May 30 to October 15.

SCHULLER MUSEUM, Farmington, N.H. Medieval arms and armor, furniture.

DANIEL WEBSTER BIRTHPLACE, on Route 127 bet. Salisbury and Franklin, N.H. Open May 30 to October 15.

WOODMAN INSTITUTE MUSEUM, DAME GARRISON HOUSE (1675) and HILTON PARK, Dover, N.H.

FRANKLIN PIERCE HOMESTEAD, Hillsboro, N.H. Open Memorial Day, then June 8 through season.

PORTSMOUTH HISTORIC HOUSES: Open mid-June to mid-September.

OTHER POINTS OF INTEREST

CURRIER GALLERY OF ART, 192 Orange St., Manchester, N.H. The state's leading art museum. Open all year.

MANCHESTER INSTITUTE OF ARTS AND SCIENCES, 148 Concord St., Manchester. Open all year.

RUGGLES MINE, on Isinglass Mountain. Off Route 4, Grafton. Open May 15 to October 15. Mineral exhibits. Oldest mica, feldspar, beryl & uranium mine in the United States.

WILDCAT VALLEY COUNTRY STORE, Jackson. Open July 1 to October 15. Old-fashioned general store of the 1880s.

CATHEDRAL OF THE PINES, Rindge. Open from Easter Sunrise service to November 17. For schedule of services, write Mrs. Reginald Hill, Exec. Director, Cathedral of the Pines Trust, Rindge, N.H.

CRAFT CENTERS OF THE LEAGUE OF N.H. ARTS AND CRAFTS are open all year in Concord, Hanover, and North Conway. Others are open in various parts of the state during the summer.

For additional information about country fairs, foliage tours, festivals and special events, write to the N.H. Division of Economic Development, Concord, N.H.

New Hampshire's Chief Executives

The following is a list of the eighty-seven men who have been chief executives, together with the title under which each served and the years in office.

Provincial Executives

Name and Residence	Title	Term	
John Cutt, Portsmouth	President	1680–81	
Richard Waldron, Dover	Deputy President	1681–82	
Edward Cranfield, London, Eng.	Lieutenant-Governor	1682–85	
Walter Barefoote, London, Eng.	Deputy-Governor	1685–86	
Joseph Dudley, Roxbury, Mass.	President, Governor	1686–87,	1702–16
Edmund Andros, London, Eng.	Governor	1687–89	
Simon Bradstreet, Salem, Mass.	Governor	1689–92	
John Usher, Boston, Mass.	Lieutenant-Governor	1692–97	
William Partridge, Portsmouth	Lieutenant-Governor	1697–98,	1701–02
Samuel Allen, London, Eng.	Governor	1698–99	
Richard Coote, Earl of Bellomont, New York	Governor	1699–1701	
Samuel Shute, Boston, Mass.	Governor	1716–23	
John Wentworth, Portsmouth	Lieutenant-Governor	1723–30	
Jonathan Belcher, Boston, Mass.	Governor	1730–41	
Benning Wentworth, Portsmouth	Governor	1741–66	
John Wentworth, Portsmouth	Governor	1767–75	

Revolutionary Executives

Matthew Thornton, Merrimack	President	1775–76	
Meshech Weare, Hampton Falls	President	1776–85	

Constitutional Executives

Name and Residence	Title	Term	
Meshech Weare, Hampton Falls	President	1784–85	
John Langdon, Portsmouth	President, Governor	1785–86,	88–89
		1805–09,	10–12
John Sullivan, Durham	President, Governor,	1786–88,	89–90
Josiah Bartlett, Kingston	President, Governor	1790–94	
John T. Gilman, Exeter	Governor	1794–1805,	13–16
Jeremiah Smith, Exeter	Governor	1809–10	
William Plumer, Epping	Governor	1812–13,	16–19
Samuel Bell, Chester	Governor	1819–23	
Levi Woodbury, Portsmouth	Governor	1823–24	
David L. Morrill, Goffstown	Governor	1824–27	
Benjamin Pierce, Hillsborough	Governor	1827–28,	29–30
John Bell, Chester	Governor	1828–29	
Matthew Harvey, Hopkinton	Governor	1830–31	
Samuel Dinsmoor, Keene	Governor	1831–34	
William Badger, Gilmanton	Governor	1834–36	
Isaac Hill, Concord	Governor	1836–39	
John Page, Haverhill	Governor	1839–42	
Henry Hubbard, Charlestown	Governor	1842–44	
John H. Steele, Peterborough	Governor	1844–46	

Anthony Colby, New London	Governor	1846–47	
Jared W. Williams, Lancaster	Governor	1847–49	
Samuel Dinsmoor, Jr., Keene	Governor	1849–52	
Noah Martin, Dover	Governor	1852–54	
Nathaniel B. Baker, Concord	Governor	1854–55	
Ralph Metcalf, Concord	Governor	1855–57	
William Haile, Hinsdale	Governor	1857–59	
Ichabod Goodwin, Portsmouth	Governor	1859–61	
Nathaniel S. Berry, Hebron	Governor	1861–63	
Joseph A. Gilmore, Concord	Governor	1863–65	
Frederick Smyth, Manchester	Governor	1865–67	
Walter Harriman, Warner	Governor	1867–69	
Onslow Stearns, Concord	Governor	1869–71	
James A. Weston, Manchester	Governor	1871–72,	74–75
Ezekiel A. Straw, Manchester	Governor	1872–74	
Person C. Cheney, Manchester	Governor	1875–77	
Benjamin F. Prescott, Epping	Governor	1877–79	
Natt Head, Hooksett	Governor	1879–81	
Charles H. Bell, Exeter	Governor	1881–83	
Samuel W. Hale, Keene	Governor	1883–85	
Moody Currier, Manchester	Governor	1885–87	
Charles H. Sawyer, Dover	Governor	1887–98	
David H. Goodell, Antrim	Governor	1889–91	
Hiram A. Tuttle, Pittsfield	Governor	1891–93	
John B. Smith, Hillsborough	Governor	1893–95	
Charles A. Busiel, Laconia	Governor	1895–97	
George A. Ramsdell, Nashua	Governor	1897–99	
Frank W. Rollins, Concord	Governor	1899–1901	
Chester B. Jordan, Lancaster	Governor	1901–03	
Nahum J. Batchelder, Andover	Governor	1903–05	
John McLane, Milford	Governor	1905–07	
Charles M. Floyd, Manchester	Governor	1907–09	
Henry B. Quinby, Laconia	Governor	1909–11	
Robert P. Bass, Peterborough	Governor	1911–13	
Samuel D. Felker, Rochester	Governor	1913–15	
Rolland H. Spaulding, Rochester	Governor	1915–17	
Henry W. Keyes, Haverhill	Governor	1917–19	
John H. Bartlett, Portsmouth	Governor	1919–21	
Albert O. Brown, Manchester	Governor	1921–23	
Fred H. Brown, Somersworth	Governor	1923–25	
John G. Winant, Concord	Governor	1925–27,	31–35
Huntley N. Spaulding, Rochester	Governor	1927–29	
Charles W. Tobey, Temple	Governor	1929–31	
H. Styles Bridges, Concord	Governor	1935–37	
Francis P. Murphy, Nashua	Governor	1937–39–41	
Robert O. Blood, Concord	Governor	1941–43–45	
Charles M. Dale, Portsmouth	Governor	1945–47–49	
Sherman Adams, Lincoln	Governor	1949–51–53	
Hugh Gregg, Nashua	Governor	1953–55	
Lane Dwinell, Lebanon	Governor	1955–59	
Wesley Powell, Hampton Falls	Governor	1959–63	
John W. King, Manchester	Governor	1963–	

Appendix B

A New Hampshire Portrait Gallery

John Stark (1728–1822)

On August 28, 1728, in a humble pioneer cabin in Londonderry, New Hampshire, John Stark was born. He was the fifth child of his parents, Archibald and Eleanor Stark. When young John was eight years old, the family moved to a new home near Amoskeag Falls in Derryfield, now known as Manchester. Here the boy grew up close to the edge of the wilderness with all its excitement and perils.

In the spring of 1752, when he was almost twenty-four years old, John Stark was with a hunting and exploring party near modern Rumney, New Hampshire. At this point he was captured by hostile Indians, and was taken prisoner to the St. Francis Indian village near Montreal. Here he was ransomed by friends from Massachusetts, and safely returned to Derryfield later that summer. The next year he was in northern New Hampshire again on a surveying expedition for the colonial authorities; and once more in 1754 he went on a similar expedition.

The French and Indian War was now beginning, and Stark became a member of '"Rogers' Rangers," the famous group of scouts that served with the British army. In 1759 he supervised the surveying of the first road across Vermont, the so-called Crown Point Road from Lake Champlain to the Connecticut River. In 1760 he left the army for a fifteen-year period of civilian life.

Having been married in 1758, ten years later John Stark built a new home for himself and his family near the Merrimack River in Derryfield. Here he lived until the outbreak of the Revolutionary War. As a farmer and a lumberman, he had numerous interests, but he was always concerned with public affairs. In 1775, immediately after the news of the British and American fighting at Lexington and Concord reached New Hampshire, he led a large company of Minutemen to Massachusetts to help the Americans there. At the Battle of Bunker Hill in June, 1775, Stark commanded the New Hampshire troops, who comprised more than half the total American forces engaged in that encounter.

In 1776 Stark and his men were in the fighting near Lake Champlain, and in late December of that year he led the advance at the Battle of Trenton. In 1777 he commanded the bulk of the forces that defeated the British army at the Battle of Bennington, and later served in the campaign around Saratoga. For these accomplishments he was eventually given the rank of Major General. As one of Washington's most dependable and trusted officers, he stayed with the army until after the final victory at Yorktown in 1781.

After the war, Stark retired to his home in Derryfield to recuperate from his long years of military service. Here he lived for forty years. In 1805 he received a most complimentary letter from President Thomas Jefferson, which closed with the words: "I salute you, venerable patriot and general. With affection and reverence." In 1809 he sent a greeting to the veterans of the Battle of Bennington, containing the words which are now the state motto of New Hampshire: "Live Free or Die." In 1814 his beloved wife of more than half a century, Elizabeth Page Stark, died, and Stark remained downcast for the rest of his life. His own death occurred in May, 1822. He was the last Major General of the Continental Army who had fought under General Washington in the winning of American Independence.

SARAH JOSEPHA HALE   (1788–1879)

Daughter of a Revolutionary War veteran from Killingworth, Connecticut, who following the war secured a 400-acre tract of land in Newport, New Hampshire, Sarah J. Buell was born on October 24, 1788. The little girl owed her education to her mother; to her brother, Horatio Buell; and to her husband. She married David Hale, a talented local lawyer in 1813, and the couple had five children. Unhappily, her husband died after nine years of marriage, leaving his widow with the children to support.

In her need to earn money Sarah Josepha Hale turned to writing. In 1827 she published a novel entitled *Northwood,* which was a great success. A year later she became editor of a Boston magazine exclusively devoted to the interests of women. By 1837 she was sufficiently well-known so that she was named editor of the *Lady's Book,* a magazine published by Louis Godey in Philadelphia. She was to hold this post with this notable periodical for forty years, and through its pages was greatly to influence American life.

While still in Boston, Mrs. Hale had demonstrated her interest in using journalism to promote public improvements. The famous Bunker Hill Monument had been started in 1825, but money for its completion was lacking. Mrs. Hale stimulated support for the project, and through various devices she helped to raise the funds needed to finish it. This was done in 1843.

After taking over the editorship of the *Lady's Book,* her public efforts multiplied. She encouraged girls and young women to go to college. She backed Elizabeth Blackwell, who received her M.D. in 1849, the first

156

woman in the U.S. ever to be admitted to the profession of medicine. She helped to start the Female Medical College of Philadelphia in 1850. She encouraged the development of the nursing profession and was happy to see the first schools for nursing in the U.S. opened in 1873. She heartily approved the use of anesthetics in surgery and urged their adoption in all hospitals. She advocated the services of women medical missionaries.

She suggested what were then termed "radical ideas" of health and sanitation. Sleeping rooms, she said, should be ventilated at night. Clothes that were too tight should be avoided. Overeating was not good for the figure or for the health of an individual. Swimming and horseback riding, even for girls, she declared, were good exercise. In 1865 she succeeded in persuading Matthew Vassar to put some of these ideas into effect in his new college just begun at Poughkeepsie, New York.

But perhaps the most famous of all her works was the composition of the poem, "Mary Had a Little Lamb." Since its first publication in 1830, it has delighted millions of children. One final accomplishment may be noted: Mrs. Hale induced President Abraham Lincoln to designate the first national Thanksgiving Day on the last Thursday of November in 1863.

SARAH HALL BOARDMAN JUDSON (1803–1845)

Driving east from North Walpole, New Hampshire, one comes to the pleasant small town of Alstead. Here in the autumn of 1803 Sarah Hall, eldest of thirteen children, was born. A devout and gentle girl, in her twenty-second year she married George Dana Boardman, a young clergyman with an ambition to become a missionary to Asia. The newly-opened country of Burma was his goal. On July 16, 1825, the couple sailed from Philadelphia; their destination was Moulmein, Burma.

The missionary movement was flourishing in our country in the years in which Sarah Hall was growing to womanhood. Beginning in 1812 the Baptists of the United States had made a great effort to send missionaries to Burma. In that year Adoniram Judson, a Massachusetts man somewhat older than the Boardmans, had sailed. His work aroused much interest among his fellow American Baptists, and the Boardmans were anxious to join him in his missionary work. Exactly as in the story of *Anna and the King of Siam*, the young couple had high hopes for the future.

But first they must learn the language. When their ship dropped them at Calcutta on December 2, 1825, almost five months from the time they had started their trip, they settled down in India to learn the language of Burma. Both Sarah and her husband mastered this difficult task so that they could read and write and speak in Burmese. In 1827 they finally reached Moulmein, Burma, and were given a warm welcome by Judson and other missionaries already there. It was a difficult place in which to work, for the Burmese of those days were not always friendly to Westerners, and the climate was a very trying one for ex-New Englanders.

Partly as a result of the conditions prevailing, George Dana Boardman died in his fourth year in Burma, leaving his young widow to continue with the effort already begun. Meantime Mrs. Judson had also died from the effects of the climate. In April, 1834, Sarah Hall Boardman and Adoniram Judson, each desirous of carrying on the missionary work, were married. In the next nine years there were eight children born of this marriage, not all of whom lived to maturity.

Mrs. Sarah Hall Boardman Judson was devoted to the art of teaching Christianity to the Burmese people. She aided her husband in putting the Bible into the language of the country, and all by herself translated *Pilgrim's Progress.* But the effort to do these things, and to care for her family was too much. In 1845 she was warned to take a rest and to return home to the United States for a well-earned vacation.

She and her husband left their missionary field and started for America by sailing around Africa. Off the western coast of that great continent lies the little island of St. Helena, famous as the last abode of the Emperor Napoleon of France who had been confined there from his exile in 1815 to his death six years later. Here on St. Helena, as the ship paused to take on food and fresh water, Sarah Hall Judson died. She was not quite forty-two years of age, and her work in Burma was far from done. She was buried on the island. Her sorrowing husband and children continued on to New England. Six years later, on another voyage, Mr. Judson also died, and he was buried at sea.

But the Christian missionary work in Burma did not stop after these brave people were gone, and more than a century later is still influencing that country.

FRANKLIN PIERCE (1804–1869)

Franklin Pierce was the only native son of New Hampshire ever to become President of the United States. He was born on November 23, 1804, in Hillsborough. Reared in a political atmosphere—his father was Governor of New Hampshire for two terms in the 1820's—Pierce attended Bowdoin College in Maine, graduating in the Class of 1824. Among his close friends there were Nathaniel Hawthorne and Henry W. Longfellow, destined to become famous writers; William Pitt Fessenden, who later became a U.S. Senator; and Calvin E. Stowe, whose wife was to write *Uncle Tom's Cabin.*

Having entered the profession of law in 1827, Pierce was married in 1834 to Jane Appleton, a member of a well-known Massachusetts family. In 1829 he was elected to the New Hampshire legislature and within two years was the Speaker of the House. In 1833 he went to Congress from his native state, serving in the House of Representatives for four years; and in 1837 he became a U.S. Senator. Elected just before his 32nd birthday, he was the youngest man ever to be chosen for that post in the history of New Hampshire. He served one term; returned to Concord to practice law; and was a military officer in the Mexican War, 1846–1848.

With so many achievements already behind him, he was nominated by his Democratic party for the Presidency in 1852. In the autumnal election that year Franklin Pierce carried twenty-seven states with an electoral vote total of 254, while his opponent carried four states with an electoral vote total of 42. It was a sweeping triumph for the man from New Hampshire. Before he and Mrs. Pierce could go to Washington to begin his term, however—in those days Presidents began their services on March 4 of the year following the election—a terrible personal tragedy struck the Pierce family. Their only surviving son, a twelve-year-old boy named Benjamin, was killed in a railroad accident. The shock was so great that for many months Mrs. Pierce felt unable to go to Washington, and her husband took the oath of office and moved into the White House alone.

Until the twentieth century Pierce was the youngest man in American history to become President. During his term of office he was anxious to keep conditions at home as calm as possible, and therefore hoped to put his emphasis on foreign affairs. He proposed a treaty with Canada which made trading between our two countries simpler. He suggested the annexation of Hawaii and the purchase of Alaska, but both ideas had to wait until later to be accomplished. He acquired more land from Mexico by the so-called Gadsden Purchase, thus filling out the modern states of Arizona and New Mexico. He sent Commodore Perry to "open Japan" in 1854, and appointed an old college friend, the Reverend Henry Wood, to be Perry's chaplain. He hoped to push American power into Cuba, but was not successful in this endeavor.

But the great issue of slavery in domestic politics could not be ignored. In many ways it continued to raise its head, and Pierce was unable to settle the issues involved. In consequence, he was not renominated by his party in 1856 and returned to New Hampshire the next year to resume the practice of law. He resided in Concord for the rest of his life. During the four years of the Civil War, his friendly attitude toward the South cost him many friends, but his essential goodness of heart and spirit prevailed through it all. His death occurred in 1869. His body was buried in Concord in a cemetery near the present Walker School.

Horace Greeley (1811–1872)

In the delightful village of Amherst, New Hampshire, a few miles west of Manchester, Horace Greeley was born on February 3, 1811. He was the third child of a farm family. The father was industrious but had little wealth or property, and, as his family increased, he kept looking for "greener pastures." When Horace was a young boy, the family moved to Poultney, Vermont, not far from Lake Champlain; and still later to Erie, Pennsylvania. In his late teens Horace Greeley, left behind in Vermont with a job when his family moved West, walked the whole distance from Poultney to Erie to rejoin them.

In 1831, carrying all his worldly possessions in a small bag, the twenty-year-old youth went to New York City to seek his fortune. He was desirous of making the newspaper business his field of activity, and amazingly enough he did just that. After holding various small jobs which earned him a little money, in 1841, ten years after his arrival in New York, he started the New York *Tribune*. It proved to be a most successful venture for him. Readers increased year by year until the newspaper had a circulation not equalled by any other American paper of the time. People all over the nation subscribed to it. It has been well said that the New York *Tribune* under Horace Greeley became a "great popular teacher," a champion of the rights of the people, and a moral influence from coast to coast.

Greeley was never satisfied with merely making money and becoming successful only in that sense. He desired also to affect the thinking of the nation. As the great Civil War began in 1861, Greeley took strong positions. From time to time he even criticized the actions of President Abraham Lincoln. Lincoln patiently tried to meet the criticisms of the strong-minded New York editor, but it was not always possible to satisfy Greeley. His paper's circulation was now approaching 300,000, and his editorial staff had many famous names on it besides his own.

After the war Greeley continued his critical attitude toward public affairs, and in 1872 allowed himself to be nominated for the Presidency by the Democratic party. Prior to this time, since the formation of the Republican party in 1856, Greeley had called himself a member of that group. But now in 1872 he amazed many of his friends by accepting the presidential nomination from the rival party. It was a hopeless campaign for Greeley. He lost the election by a great majority of electoral and popular votes. Even worse than that, on October 30, 1872, his wife died, leaving him utterly bereaved. Worn out by the shock of his wife's death and by his overwhelming loss at the polls, Greeley himself sickened and died on November 29, 1872.

This remarkable man will always have a high place in the history of American journalism. He brought to the newspaper world new standards, new ideas, and a new concept of the power of a newspaper. At the peak of his career with the New York *Tribune* he had the gift of striking off slogans and expressions which made him famous. His well-known "Go West, young man, go West," became a challenge and inspiration to thousands of Americans to leave the eastern states and search out new homes in the Rocky Mountain area and along the Pacific Coast. As long as people read newspapers, many will remember the name of Horace Greeley.

Mary Baker Eddy (1821–1910)

To Mary Baker Eddy, born in Bow, New Hampshire, on July 16, 1821, is to be credited the achievement of founding an entirely new religious denomination in our country. This faith is known as Christian Science. Its rise and growth are a remarkable tribute to the unusual woman who began it.

Mary Baker Eddy, whose birthplace in Bow is now marked, showing the foundation of the original homestead, was the youngest of six children. When she was fifteen years of age, her parents moved their family to Tilton, a few miles north and east. Even at this age, Mary Baker had a deep interest in theology, which later opened into her life work.

Here in Tilton, in 1843, when she was twenty-two years old, she was married; but, as she writes in her own biography, "he (Colonel George Washington Glover) was spared to me for only one brief year." After his death their son was born, also in Tilton. When the boy, George, was five years old, and because of Mary's ill health, he was sent to live with her sister Abigail and later with a former nurse. Several years later Dr. Daniel Patterson, a dentist, offered her marriage and she accepted; but at no time would he consider having George with them, and after some years she divorced him in 1873.

During their years of separation Mrs. Patterson earned her living by her writing, while living quietly with her sister. Then, in February of 1866, she healed herself by prayer from what the doctor had considered a fatal injury from a fall on the ice. Out of this experience was born Christian Science. In 1875 Mary Baker published her textbook, *Science and Health with Key to the Scriptures,* designed to teach others to help themselves. This book has been translated into many languages and is read and studied by countless people throughout the world.

In 1877 Mary married for the third time; her husband was Asa G. Eddy. In 1879 Mrs. Eddy officially founded the Church of Christ, Scientist, with twenty-six members, and in 1892 she authorized the building of The Mother Church in Boston. The first meeting was held in this beautiful stone structure on December 30, 1894. The following week it was dedicated, having been completely paid for by contributions from its members. An extension to this Church, a magnificent building with seating capacity for about five thousand people, was finished and dedicated in 1906. Two years later, in 1908, Mrs. Eddy founded *The Christian Science Monitor* which has since become one of the best-known newspapers in the United States.

From 1889 to 1908 she wrote extensively and governed the great growth of the Christian Science movement while living on her estate in Concord, New Hampshire, not far from her birthplace. Ten thousand of her followers congregated on her lawn, in 1903, to hear her address them, and in that year Mrs. Eddy provided the funds for the beautiful church building still standing in the capital city of our state.

Her last two years were spent in Chestnut Hill, near Boston, where she passed on December 3, 1910. She was buried in Mt. Auburn Cemetery in Cambridge, Massachusetts.

Mary Baker Eddy is remembered and admired by people all over the world. Her deep religious conviction of spiritual healing has brought comfort to thousands.

LAURA BRIDGMAN   (1829–1889)

In the famous New Hampshire town of Hanover Laura Dewey Bridgman was born during Christmas week of 1829. At the age of two she suffered an attack of scarlet fever which left her with both sight and hearing destroyed. Since this happened before she had learned to talk, she was unable to speak. Hence to her parents and friends, the future of the little girl seemed very black indeed. She was blind; she was deaf; and she was speechless.

In 1831 a noted American doctor named Samuel Gridley Howe had started in Boston a school for the blind which he called the Perkins Institute. Dr. Howe had travelled in Europe and had been impressed with some of the new ideas which teachers on that continent were developing to help people who were lacking in any of their five senses, but especially sight and hearing. In 1837, on a visit to Hanover, Dr. Howe heard of the afflictions which had come to Laura Bridgman and persuaded her parents to let him take the little girl back to Boston with him for treatment there.

After years of training, Laura was taught how to do many things which normal children can do. While she could never see nor hear in the true sense, she learned to read raised letters—Braille, we would call it today; she learned to sew; and she could speak so that others could easily understand her words. Dr. Howe was tremendously proud of his prize pupil, for Laura Bridgman was the first child in America to overcome such handicaps, and by systematic education she was able to do many of the things that others can do.

In 1852 Laura tried the experiment of going back to her home in Hanover, but she was not happy there. She loved the life of the Perkins Institute, and soon returned to that place, remaining there for the rest of her life. She was a great favorite with all the other patients in the Institute and was one of the teachers in the sewing class. It is said that her work as a seamstress was so perfect that it excelled that of many people with normal vision.

When the English writer, Charles Dickens, visited the United States on a trip to this country in 1842, he met the young girl, Laura Bridgman. Later in one of his books Dickens wrote that his two most vivid memories of America were Laura Bridgman and Niagara Falls! Certainly this was a rare compliment to the blind and deaf girl. Dr. Howe, her favorite teacher, always spoke of her with pride. He praised what he called ". . . her unfailing good spirits, her affections, and her passion for life."

Most people today have heard of the great modern American woman named Helen Keller. It is sometimes forgotten that Miss Keller was taught by the same methods which had been devised for the instruction of Laura Bridgman, and her own accomplishment owes much to the effort of this earlier woman. No wonder that in the beautiful Congregational Church of Hanover, New Hampshire, today one of the most impressive rooms is known as the Laura Bridgman Room. It will always commemorate for us the life and achievement of one of the great women of our state.

Thaddeus S. C. Lowe (1832–1913)

In the middle of the nineteenth century interest in ballooning was as keen among scientific people and the public in general as the desire to conquer outer space is today. One of the Americans who did much in this field was Thaddeus S. C. Lowe, born in Randolph, New Hampshire, in 1832. Lowe became interested in the use of balloons in his late teens, and by the time he was twenty-four years old their development was his master passion. In 1858 he was making ascensions by balloon in Canada; the next year he was in New York building a balloon which he named "The City of New York." This was a huge affair, measuring 130 feet in diameter, and estimated to have a lifting power of more than twenty tons.

163

Well aware that the prevailing winds in the United States come from the west, Lowe was anxious to try to drift across the Atlantic Ocean on westerly winds all the way from New York to Europe. Before attempting this, however, his friends advised him to see how far he could go over land. In the spring of 1861, therefore, he journeyed to Cincinnati, Ohio, and on the morning of April 20 cast off. Nine hours later and several hundred miles away in South Carolina, his balloon came to earth. He had drifted to the east, it was true, but the distance travelled was much shorter than a transatlantic crossing.

As soon as the Civil War started Lowe promptly betook himself to Washington to offer his services to his country. He had in mind establishing a kind of Balloon Corps, whose duties would be to make military observations from the air, and to report these by telegraph wires attached to the anchor cables. On the 18th of June, 1861, from a balloon anchored 1000 feet in the air, with President Lincoln watching the experiment, Lowe sent a telegram from his aircraft to the earth. This was the first time that such a transmission had ever been made.

In August, 1861, Lowe was made Military Aeronaut of the Union Army in the East and directed to construct five balloons. These he built in the next few months, naming them "Eagle," "Washington," "Constitution," "Intrepid," and "Union." The balloons, filled with hydrogen gas, could lift Lowe or one of his assistants as high as 2500 feet, making possible accurate visual observations. Likewise, Lowe utilized the new invention of photography to take pictures of the ground underneath, to be forwarded to the army commanders. The Confederate forces were much annoyed by these Union observation balloons, but were never successful in shooting down any of them.

Because of ill health, in 1863 Lowe had to discontinue his balloon work for the army. He still maintained his interest in it, however, and in 1865 performed the first aerial wedding in American history in a balloon anchored in Central Park, New York. The next year he was in Brazil, showing the ruler of that country how to make balloons work. In later years he turned his attention to the manufacture of artificial ice and the improvement of gas manufacture. In each area he was most successful. For instance, in 1868 he transported frozen beef from the Gulf of Mexico with no spoilage of the meat or damage to its eating quality. In his last years he lived in Pasadena, California, where he died in 1913. A mountain near that city is still called Mt. Lowe.

In his insistence that air could be conquered and used by and for human beings, Thaddeus S. C. Lowe was much ahead of his time. But his feeling was correct, and we in the twentieth century can best appreciate what a farsighted man he truly was.

CELIA LAIGHTON THAXTER   (1835–1894)

Off the seacoast of New Hampshire lie nine small islands known collectively as the Isles of Shoals. They are called Duck, Appledore, Malaga, Smuttynose, Cedar (these five belonging to the State of Maine); and Star, Lunging, White, and Seavey (these four belonging to the State of New Hampshire). The total area of all nine is not quite half a square mile, and yet for hundreds of years they have been objects of interest to many people.

Celia Laighton through her writings about the islands and Thomas Laighton, her father, through his summer hotel on Appledore, helped to make the islands popular as a summer resort and even famous. In 1839 Thomas Laighton was appointed keeper of the lighthouse on the Isles of Shoals, and in October of that year he moved his family to the keeper's house on White Island. Here Celia and her brothers grew up, with ample opportunity to enjoy the natural beauties of the islands. In 1848 Thomas Laighton opened the summer hotel on Appledore which became the first resort hotel on the New England seacoast. There Celia met visitors like James Russell Lowell, John Greenleaf Whittier, and many other writers and artists of the day.

In September, 1851, when just past sixteen years of age, Celia was married to Levi Lincoln Thaxter, who had also been a summer visitor. For some years thereafter she lived at least part of each year in Newtonville, Massachusetts. Due to the illnesses of her parents, however, and her husband's need for a warmer climate, she was forever torn between the two families, traveling frequently between Massachusetts and the Isles of Shoals in all weathers. She helped her father and brothers with the running of Appledore House for many years.

In 1859 Celia Thaxter wrote a poem entitled "Land-locked" about her longing for the sea and the islands, which was printed in the *Atlantic Monthly*. Her husband had shown the verses to James Russell Lowell, the editor, without her knowledge. Encouraged by this and by her friends' praise and especially by Whittier, who became a long-time friend and critic, Celia continued to express herself in poetry and in prose. *Among the Isles of Shoals,* the book for which she is most famous, was published in 1873. It made her well known on both sides of the Atlantic.

Among the poets she most admired was Robert Browning. When Celia Thaxter went abroad for the first time in the autumn of 1880 with her brother, she met Browning in England just before returning home. To meet him and talk as one poet to another was a great experience for her. A nature poem characteristic of her own writing that Browning liked was called "One Little Sandpiper and I." It told of her thoughts as she watched the bird on a lonely stretch of beach and of her feelings as she looked over the islands and the broad ocean.

In 1884 her husband died. Mrs. Thaxter lived another ten years writing and expanding the many friendships she had made. She died on the islands she so much loved and was buried on Appledore. Every summer hundreds of people take the boat from Portsmouth to the Isles of Shoals and seek out the places described in her writings. Conferences are held in the little stone chapel near her former home, and the remnants of her once flourishing garden and other loved places on the island are admired by today's visitors. Celia Laighton Thaxter was the chief woman poet in the history of New Hampshire, and it is well that her name is remembered.

ERNEST MARTIN HOPKINS (1877—)

Ernest Martin Hopkins was born in the historic town of Dunbarton, New Hampshire, twelve years after the close of the Civil War. As these lines are being written he is still alive and active in many endeavors. His father was named Adoniram Judson Hopkins, thus honoring the famous missionary already mentioned. Young Ernest went to Worcester Academy in Massachusetts and then attended Dartmouth College at Hanover. He took his degree at Dartmouth in the Class of 1901, just a hundred years after the graduation of one of Dartmouth's most famous alumni, Daniel Webster.

Dartmouth College, founded in 1769, is the ninth oldest college in the United States. For almost a century it had been the only institution of higher learning in New Hampshire, the University not being founded until 1866. During this long period when it was the only college in the state, Dartmouth built up many proud traditions and a devoted body of alumni. Ernest Hopkins was to carry on these traditions and stimulate the interest of the alumni to an extent that no previous president of Dartmouth ever had accomplished.

In 1901 he began a four-year term as secretary to the then president of Dartmouth. In 1905 he began a five-year term as Secretary to the College. In 1916 he came back to the campus as President of Dartmouth, a position which he held with great distinction for the next twenty-nine years. During his few years away from Hanover he engaged in special work for various large industrial concerns and gained a wide acquaintance with American businessmen and their thinking. These friendships and special knowledge were to aid President Hopkins during the years when Dartmouth was expanding so successfully.

Somehow this busy college president found time to do much work for his country in fields far removed from the campus at Hanover. During

World War I he was an assistant to the Secretary of War, in charge of industrial relations. Just before World War II he was serving in the Office of Production Management in Washington. In 1933 he worked on a special assignment for the government in Puerto Rico, and in 1947 he had a somewhat similar duty to perform in Guam and Samoa. In 1948 he became president of the National Life Insurance Company of Montpelier, Vermont. In addition to these manifold tasks, he did special work for the Rockefeller Foundation and served on the boards of directors of many business corporations and schools.

But most of all "Hoppy," as his alumni loved to call him, was devoted to Dartmouth. He travelled the country from coast to coast, meeting with the graduates and keeping alive their pride in the college. He secured money to build many of the fine buildings which now are part of the Dartmouth campus. He encouraged the growth of athletics and the outdoor activities for which Dartmouth is famous. He kept the college in touch with the changing currents of American education and developed not only a great library and modern laboratories but a fine faculty.

Today his name is commemorated by the Hopkins Fine Arts Center at Dartmouth, an impressive building dedicated in 1962. In this beautiful and unusual structure are housed many activities, and in its auditoriums are held many programs. Ernest Martin Hopkins is still able to enjoy the life of the college over which he presided as president from 1916 to 1945. His is a great name in American education.

Bibliography

For Chapter One

BROWN, WILLIAM R., *Our Forest Heritage*. Concord, N.H., New Hampshire Historical Society, 1958.

RICHARDS, TUDOR, *List of the Birds in New Hampshire*. Concord, N.H., Audubon Society of New Hampshire, 1959.

SEIGLER, HILBERT N., *New Hampshire Nature Notes*. Orford, N.H., Equity Publishing Company, 1962.

SILVER, HELENETTE, *A History of New Hampshire Game and Fur Bearers*. Concord, N.H., Evans Printing Company, 1957.

SMITH, R. V., "New Hampshire Remembers the Indians," *Historical New Hampshire*, October, 1952.

THOMPSON, BETTY FLANDERS, *The Changing Face of New England*. New York, Macmillan, 1958.

For Chapter Two

BAKELESS, JOHN, *The Eyes of Discovery*. Philadelphia, Dover, 1951.

BARKER, SHIRLEY, *Rivers Parting*. New York, Crown Publishers, 1950.

BROWN, W. H., *Colonel John Goffe*. Glens Falls, N.Y., The Author, 1950.

HUNT, E. H., "Our New Hampshire Scotch Settlers," *Historical New Hampshire*, November, 1944.

PECKHAM, HOWARD H., *Captured by Indians*. New Brunswick, Rutgers University Press, 1954.

POHL, FREDERICK J., *Atlantic Crossings Before Columbus*. New York, Norton, 1961.

For Chapter Three

GOULD, MARY EARLE, *Early American Woodenware and Other Kitchen Utensils*. Rutland, Vt., Charles E. Tuttle Co., 1962.

MAYO, LAWRENCE S., *John Wentworth, Governor of New Hampshire*. Cambridge, Mass., Harvard University Press, 1921.

PICHIERRE, LOUIS, *Music in New Hampshire, 1623–1800*. New York, Columbia University Press, 1960.

RICHARDSON, L. B., *History of Dartmouth College*. Hanover, N.H., Dartmouth College Press, 1932.

SALTONSTALL, WILLIAM G., *Ports of Piscataqua*. Cambridge, Mass., Harvard University Press, 1941.

SHURTLEFF, H. R., *The Log Cabin Myth*. Cambridge, Mass., Harvard University Press, 1939.

[1] SPEARE, EVA A., *Colonial Meeting-Houses of New Hampshire*. Plymouth, N.H., Privately printed, 1938.

WOODBURY, GEORGE W., *John Goffe's Mill*. New York, W. W. Norton & Co., 1948.

W.P.A. WRITERS PROJECT, *Hands That Built New Hampshire*. Brattleboro, Vt., Stephen Daye Press, 1940.

For Chapter Four

HAMMOND, OTIS G., *The History of the Seal and Flag of the State of New Hampshire*. Concord, N.H., Historical Society, 1916.

KETCHUM, ALTON, *Uncle Sam, The Man and the Legend*. New York, Hill and Wang, Inc., 1959.

MAYO, LAWRENCE S., *John Langdon of New Hampshire*. Concord, N.H., The Rumford Press, 1937.

MOORE, HOWARD P., *A Life of General John Stark of New Hampshire*. New York, Privately printed, 1949.

PAGE, ELWIN L., *George Washington in New Hampshire*. Boston, Houghton Mifflin Company, 1932.

[3] UPTON, RICHARD F., *Meshech Weare, 1713–1786*. Exeter, N.H., New Hampshire Society of Colonial Wars, 1960.

[2] UPTON, RICHARD F., *Revolutionary New Hampshire*. Hanover, N.H., Dartmouth College Press, 1936.

WHITTEMORE, CHARLES P., *A General of the Revolution: John Sullivan of New Hampshire*. New York, Columbia University Press, 1961.

For Chapter Five

BROWN, R. H., *The Struggle for the Indian Stream Territory*. Cleveland, Western Reserve University Press, 1955.

BURGUM, EDWIN J., *The Concord Coach*. Concord, N.H., Rumford Press, 1939.

CALDWELL, W. H., *The Guernsey*. Peterborough, N.H., American Guernsey Cattle Club, 1941.

FUESS, CLAUDE M., *Daniel Webster*. 2 vols. Boston, Little, Brown & Co., 1930.

[4] MELCHER, MARGUERITE, *The Shaker Adventure*. Princeton, Princeton University Press, 1941.

NICHOLS, ROY F., *Franklin Pierce: Young Hickory of the Granite Hills*. 2nd ed., revised. Philadelphia, University of Pennsylvania Press, 1958.

TURNER, LYNN W., *William Plumer of New Hampshire, 1759–1850*. Chapel Hill, University of North Carolina Press, 1962.

WATERMAN, W. R., "The Fourth New Hampshire Turnpike," *Historical New Hampshire*, XV, November, 1960.

WILSON, HAROLD F., *The Hill Country of Northern New England: Its Social and Economic History, 1790–1930*. New York, Columbia University Press, 1936.

For Chapter Six

BLOOD, GRACE H., *Manchester on the Merrimack*. Manchester, N.H., Lew A. Cummings Co., 1948.

GOODRICH, CARTER, *Government Promotion of Canals and Railroads, 1800–1890*. New York, Columbia University Press, 1960.

HARLOW, ALVIN F., *Steelways of New England*. New York, Creative Age Press, 1946.

KIRKLAND, EDWARD C., *Men, Cities, and Transportation*. Cambridge, Harvard University Press, 1948.

REED, R. T., *American Express: Its Origin and Growth*. Princeton, Princeton University Press, 1952.

SQUIRES, J. DUANE, *The Northern Railroad of New Hampshire, 1844–1848*. Princeton, Princeton University Press, 1948.

[5] STRAW, WILLIAM P., *Amoskeag in New Hampshire: An Epic in American Industry*. Princeton, Princeton University Press, 1948.

[6] SULLOWAY, RICHARD W., "New Hampshire's Part in the Evolution of Modern Knitting Machinery," *Historical New Hampshire*, XI, December, 1956.

VAN DEUSEN, GLYNDON G., *Horace Greeley, Nineteenth Century Crusader*. Philadelphia, University of Pennsylvania Press, 1953.

WOODBURY, GEORGE, *John Goffe's Legacy*. New York, W. W. Norton and Co., 1955.

For Chapter Seven

BROOKS, VAN WYCK, *The Flowering of New England, 1815–1865*. New York, E. P. Dutton & Co., 1936.

FINLEY, RUTH, *The Lady of Godey's Book*. Philadelphia, J. B. Lippincott, 1931.

JORDAN, PHILIP D., *Singin' Yankees*. Minneapolis, University of Minnesota Press, 1946.

LATOURETTE, KENNETH S., *Missions and the American Mind*. Indianapolis, Bobbs-Merrill Co., 1949.

KINNEY, CHARLES B., *Church and State in New Hampshire*. New York, Columbia University Press, 1954.

[7] MCSWEENEY, ANNE M., Article in *New Hampshire Profiles*, September, 1954.

SHERA, J. H., *The Origins of the Public Library Movement in New England, 1629–1855*. Chicago, University of Chicago Press, 1949.

SQUIRES, J. DUANE, *A History of the YMCA in New Hampshire to 1944*. Concord, N.H., Concord Press, 1944.

THAXTER, ROSAMOND, *Sandpiper: The Life of Celia Thaxter*, Francestown, N.H., Marshall Jones Co., 1963.

TYLER, ALICE F., *Freedom's Ferment*. Minneapolis, University of Minnesota Press, 1944.

WADE, MASON, *The Journals of Francis Parkman*. 2 vols. New York, Harper & Brothers, 1947.

For Chapter Eight

ADAMS, G. W., *Doctors in Blue*. New York, Henry Schuman, Inc., 1952.

DONALD, DAVID, ed. *Inside Lincoln's Cabinet: The Civil War Diaries of Salmon P. Chase*. New York, Longmans, Green and Co., 1954.

GREENBIE, MARJORIE, *Lincoln's Daughters of Mercy*. New York, G. P. Putnam's Sons, 1944.

HESSELTINE, W. B., *Lincoln and the War Governors*. New York, Alfred A. Knopf, 1948.

MARSTON, PHILIP M., "Amos Tuck and the Beginning in New Hampshire of the Republican Party," *Historical New Hampshire*, XV, November, 1960.

PAGE, ELWIN L., *Abraham Lincoln in New Hampshire*. Boston, Houghton Mifflin Co., 1929.

RICHARDSON, L. B., *William E. Chandler: Republican*. New York, Dodd, Mead and Company, 1940.

SQUIRES, J. DUANE, "Aeronautics in the Civil War," *American Historical Review*, XLII, July, 1937.

SQUIRES, J. DUANE, "Mrs. Abraham Lincoln's Visit to Mount Washington in 1863," *Appalachia*, XXXIII, December 15, 1961.

WILEY, BELL I., *The Life of Billy Yank*. Indianapolis, Bobbs-Merrill Company, 1951.

For Chapter Nine

BLOOD, GRACE H., *Manchester on the Merrimack*. Manchester, N.H., Lew A. Cummings Company, 1948.

BUFFUM, F. H., ed., *New Hampshire and the Federal Constitution.* Concord, N.H., Rumford Press, 1940.

CLARK, EUGENE F., ed., *War Record of Dartmouth College, 1917–1918.* Hanover, N.H., Dartmouth College Press, 1922.

9 GUYOL, PHILIP, *Democracy Fights: A History of New Hampshire in World War II.* Hanover, N.H., Dartmouth College Press, 1951.

HESSELTINE, W. B., *The Rise and Fall of Third Parties.* Madison, The University of Wisconsin Press, 1948.

8 JOHNSON, ETHEL M., in "The Mr. Winant I Knew," *South Atlantic Quarterly,* January, 1949.

PILLSBURY, HOBART, *New Hampshire: Resources, Attractions, and Its People.* New York, American Historical Company, 1927.

RICHARDSON, L. B., *William E. Chandler: Republican.* New York, Dodd, Mead and Company, 1940.

STACKPOLE, E. S., *History of New Hampshire.* New York, American Historical Company, 1916.

SULLIVAN, MARK, *Our Times: Over Here, 1914–1918.* New York, Charles Scribner's Sons, 1933.

WILSON, EDITH, *My Memoir.* New York, Bobbs-Merrill, 1939.

W.P.A. WRITERS PROJECT, *New Hampshire: A Guide to the Granite State.* Boston, Houghton Mifflin Company, 1938.

For Chapter Ten

BLOOD, GRACE H., *Manchester on the Merrimack.* Manchester, N.H., Lew A. Cummings Co., 1948.

BURT, F. ALLEN, *The Story of Mount Washington.* Hanover, N.H., Dartmouth College Press, 1960.

DREIER, THOMAS A., *Sunny Meadows.* Boston, The Stratford Co., 1933.

11 DOWLING, L. H., in *New Hampshire Profiles,* May, 1952.

HANDLIN, OSCAR, *The Uprooted.* Cambridge, Harvard University Press, 1953.

MITCHELL, E. V., *The Horse and Buggy Age in New England.* New York, Coward-McCann Inc., 1937.

NEALE, R. M., *High Green and Bark Peelers.* New York, Duell, Sloan and Pearce, 1950.

SLOANE, ERIC, *American Barns and Covered Bridges.* New York, Wilfred Funk Inc., 1954.

SQUIRES, J. DUANE, *Mirror to America: A History of New London, New Hampshire, 1900–1950.* Concord, N.H., Evans Press, 1952.

WADE, MASON, *The French Canadians, 1760–1945.* New York, The Macmillan Company, 1955.

10 WILSON, HAROLD F., *The Hill Country of Northern New England: Its*

Social and Economic History, 1790–1930. New York, Columbia University Press, 1936.

WOODBURY, GEORGE, *The Story of a Stanley Steamer*. New York, W. W. Norton and Company, 1950.

For Chapter Eleven

BABCOCK, DONALD C., *New England Harvest*. Bloomington, Ind., Indiana University Press, 1953.

BEASLEY, NORMAN, *The Cross and the Crown*. Boston, Little, Brown and Company, 1952.

BULLARD, F. LAURISTON, *Lincoln in Marble and Bronze*. New Brunswick, N.J., Rutgers University Press, 1952.

BENÉT, STEPHEN VINCENT, *The Devil and Daniel Webster*. New York, Farrar and Rinehart, Inc., 1937.

CHILDS, FRANCIS LANE, ed., *New Hampshire: A Bicentennial Book*. Brattleboro, Vt., Vermont Printing Company, 1961.

CRESSON, MARGARET FRENCH, *Journey Into Fame: The Life of Daniel Chester French*. Cambridge, Harvard University Press, 1947.

HARRISON, ALICE S., ed., *A History of the New Hampshire Federation of Women's Clubs, 1895–1940*. Bristol, N.H., Musgrove Printing House, 1941.

History of the University of New Hampshire, 1866–1941. Rochester, N.H., The Record Press, 1941.

MONAHAN, R. S., *Mt. Washington Reoccupied*. Brattleboro, Vt., Vermont Printing Company, 1933.

The New England Economy: A Report to the President. Washington, Government Printing Office, 1951.

For Chapter Twelve

ADAMS, SHERMAN, *First-Hand Report: The Story of the Eisenhower Administration*. New York, Harper and Brothers, 1961.

BLACK, JOHN D., *The Rural Economy of New England*. Cambridge, Harvard University Press, 1950.

BRIGHT, ARTHUR A. and ELLIS, GEORGE H., *The Economic State of New England*. New Haven, Yale University Press, 1954.

Directory of General Welfare Resources of New Hampshire. Concord, N.H., Rumford Press, 1948.

HARRIS, SEYMOUR E., *Economics of New England*. Cambridge, Harvard University Press, 1952.

HOUSTON, CHARLES S. and BATES, ROBERT H., *K-2—The Savage Mountain*. New York, McGraw-Hill Book Co., Inc., 1954.

LEUCHTENBURG, WILLIAM E., *The Connecticut Valley Problem, 1927–1950.*
Cambridge, Harvard University Press, 1950.

New Hampshire Notables. Concord, N.H., Concord Press, 1955.

SMITH, EARL L., *Yankee Genius: A Biography of Roger Babson.* New York,
Harper and Brothers, 1954.

WHITE, WILLIAM L., *Lost Boundaries.* New York, Harcourt, Brace & World,
Inc., 1948.

FOR FURTHER READING

FICTION FOR YOUNG PEOPLE

THE STORY OF A BAD BOY   Thomas Bailey Aldrich
Autobiography of a Portsmouth, N.H., lad, slightly concealed by
changes in names and places. A nineteenth century classic.
(Houghton, 1923, Pantheon, 1951)

LITTLE RED SCHOOLHOUSE   Carolyn S. Bailey
A city boy learns the joys of a two-room country school near
Temple, N.H., as well as independence and cooperation. (Viking
Press, 1957)

MISS HICKORY   Carolyn S. Bailey
The story of a hickory nut doll who lives in outdoor New Hampshire. (Viking Press, 1946)

DOWN THE MAST ROAD   John M. Duncan
Story of Revolutionary times when the giant white pines of New
Hampshire were cut for masts for the King's Navy. (McGraw,
1956)

THE DEVIL AND DANIEL WEBSTER   Stephen Vincent Benet
A tale of New Hampshire's famous son that is considered a
classic. (Holt, Rinehart & Winston, 1937)

CANDIDATE FOR TRUTH   Sybil Norton and John Cournos
A story of Daniel Webster. (Holt, Rinehart & Winston, 1953)

MYSTERY AT THE SHOALS   Duane Bradley
A mystery treasure hunt on one of the Isles of Shoals. (Lippincott,
1962)

OCEAN-BORN MARY   Lois Lenski
A legend furnishes the inspiration for this picture of Portsmouth,
N.H., in colonial times. (Lippincott. 1939)

GALLANT WARRIOR   Helen R. Mann
A fictionalized interpretation of the records concerning Hannah

Duston who slew her Indian captors at a point near Concord, New Hampshire. (Eerdmans, 1954)

WHO RIDES IN THE DARK? Stephen Meader
Dan, the stable boy at the "Fox and Stars," plays a major part in the capture of a robber gang in old stagecoach days in southern New Hampshire. (Harcourt, Brace & World, 1937)

OLD PEPPERSASS Leonard A. Stevens
The Locomotive That Climbed Mount Washington. Fictional version, especially for boys, of the building of the railroad up the mountain. Based on true history. (Dodd, Mead, 1959)

AS THE WHEEL TURNS Anne Tufts
An exciting story of Quakers and of the beginning of the textile industry in N.H. (Holt, 1952) o. p.

PATTERNS ON THE WALL Elizabeth Yates
The story of an itinerant painter who stenciled walls of New Hampshire homes in the early 19th century and of the girl he loved. (Dutton, 1953)

ADULT FICTION

LOOK TO THE MOUNTAIN LeGrand Cannon, Jr.
A moving love story of pioneer life in Tamworth, N.H. (Holt, Rinehart & Winston, 1942)

BIOGRAPHY

FIRST WOMAN EDITOR, SARAH JOSEPHA HALE Olive W. Burt
(Messner, 1960)

SPREAD THE TRUTH: THE LIFE OF HORACE GREELEY W. J. Granberg
Concerned mainly with Greeley's early life in New Hampshire and Vermont, and briefly with his life in New York City. (Dutton, 1959)

THADDEUS LOWE: AMERICA'S ONE-MAN AIR CORPS Mary D. Hoehling
(Messner, 1958)

SAMUEL MORSE AND THE TELEGRAPH Wilma Pitchford Hays
(Watts, 1960)

FIGHTING YANKEE Robert E. Pike
The childhood and early manhood of General John Stark, including his many exciting adventures in the French and Indian War. (Abelard, 1955)

DANIEL WEBSTER Alfred Steinberg
A complete and readable biography which also explains the principles on which our country was founded. (Putnam, 1959)

SANDPIPER   Rosamond Thaxter
    The life and letters of Celia Thaxter edited by her granddaughter.
    (Marshall Jones, 1963)
AMOS FORTUNE, FREE MAN   Elizabeth Yates
    A remarkable man who once lived in Jaffrey, Amos Fortune was
    born free, but became a slave and had to buy his freedom. At his
    death he left a gift for all to share. (Dutton, 1950)

NON-FICTION

A LIST OF THE BIRDS OF NEW HAMPSHIRE   Tudor Richards
    Does not include descriptions, but gives seasonal residence,
    habitat, geographical distribution and relative abundance. (Au-
    dubon Society of New Hampshire)
TREES AND SHRUBS OF NEW HAMPSHIRE   John H. Foster
    A handbook giving varieties of trees and shrubs found in the state,
    grouped by families. (Society for the Protection of N.H. Forests,
    1960)
AN OLD TOWN BY THE SEA   Thomas Bailey Aldrich
    The author's native town, Portsmouth, N.H., its history, old
    houses, and personalities recalled. (Houghton, 1893, o. p.)
AMONG THE ISLES OF SHOALS   Celia Thaxter
    The 19th century poetess, Celia Thaxter, spent most of her life
    on Appledore, one of the Isles of Shoals, when it was a popular
    summer resort frequented by literary figures of the day. (Wake-
    Brook Press, 1962)
NEW HAMPSHIRE NATURE NOTES   Hilbert R. Siegler
    Though not confined to New Hampshire alone, the wild life
    described so expertly in this book is typical of the region. (Equity
    Publishing, 1962)

Other resources are listed in the Bibliography of this book, beginning on
page 169. Also the New Hampshire State Library, Concord, New Hampshire, provides selected reading lists of books about New Hampshire from
time to time. We are indebted to this library and to Mrs. Lois R. Markey,
Librarian, Concord Public Library, Concord, N.H., for suggestions for
the above reading list.

Index

Biography of J. Duane Squires

At the age of seven J. Duane Squires undertook his first historical writing. It was a book review of Noah Brooks' *The Boy Emigrants*. In more recent years he has published six books, scores of articles in historical journals, and hundreds of book reviews.

Born in North Dakota, in 1933 he and his wife, Catherine —he married his high school sweetheart in 1928—moved to New Hampshire. This move came immediately after his attaining the Ph.D. at Harvard University. Since then, he has been chairman of the Department of Social Studies at Colby Junior College. During his thirty years on campus, he has had more than 4500 students in his classes, with many of whom he still keeps in touch. He and his wife have two married sons, one a lawyer, the other an M.D., and three grandchildren.

Duane and Catherine Squires have been active in many local, state, and national groups. He was an elected New Hampshire delegate to the national Republican conventions of 1952 and 1956. He was an appointed delegate from the American Baptist Convention to the World Council of Churches Assembly of 1954. He has served as president or chairman of more than a dozen local and statewide organizations, and is now Municipal Judge of the Town of New London.

In 1961 he and his wife spent four months in Western Europe, studying international institutions: NATO, European Common Market, the International Court of Justice, and the specialized agencies of the U.N. His hobbies are golf, gardening, and occasional fishing.